For Kooler Design Studio, Inc.

President: Donna Kooler
Executive Vice President: Linda Gillum
Vice President: Priscilla Timm
Editor: Deanna Hall West
Associate Editor: Kit Schlich
Contributing Editor: Priscilla Timm
Designers: Linda Gillum, Nancy Rossi, Barbara Baatz,
Sandy Orton, Jorja Hernandez, Tom Taneyhill
Design Assistants: Sara Angle, Jennifer Drake,
Anita Forfang, Virginia Hanley-Rivett, Marsha Hinkson,
Lisa Justice, Lori Patten, Char Randolph, Giana Shaw,
Lois Tedeso.
Project Finishing: Laurie Grant

Dedication

My love and grateful thanks to CRW and JBW, my
sons and first stitching students, and to VHH, my
mother and first stitching teacher.

Deanna Hall West

Library of Congress Cataloging-in-Publication Data Available

Kooler, Donna.
    Cross-stitch for the first time / Donna Kooler.
       p. cm.
    "A Sterling/Chapelle Book."
    ISBN 0-8069-1963-9
    1. Cross-stitch. I. Title.

TT778.C76. K662 2000
746.44'3--dc21   00-037049

10   9   8   7   6   5   4   3   2   1

Published by Sterling Publishing Company, Inc.
387 Park Avenue South, New York, N.Y. 10016
© 2000 by Kooler Design Studios
Distributed in Canada by Sterling Publishing
c/o Canadian Manda Group, One Atlantic Avenue, Suite 105
Toronto, Ontario, Canada M6K 3E7
Distributed in Great Britain and Europe by Cassell PLC
Wellington House, 125 Strand, London WC2R 0BB, England
Distributed in Australia by Capricorn Link (Australia) Pty Ltd.
P.O. Box 6651, Baulkham Hills, Business Centre, NSW 2153, Australia
Printed in China
All rights reserved

Sterling ISBN 0-8069-1963-9

For Chapelle Limited

Owner: Jo Packham
Editor: Ann Bear

Staff: Areta Bingham, Kass Burchett, Marilyn Goff,
Holly Hollingsworth, Susan Jorgensen, Barbara Milburn,
Linda Orton, Karmen Quinney, Leslie Ridenour,
Cindy Stoeckl, Gina Swapp

Photography: Kevin Dilley for Hazen Imaging, Inc.
Photo styling: Jo Packham

Special Thanks

We would like to offer our sincere appreciation of the
valuable support given in this ever-changing industry of
new ideas, concepts, designs, and products. Several
projects shown in this publication were created with the
outstanding and innovative products developed by:

DMC:
10 Port Kearney Building; South Dearney, NJ 07032-4688

Kreinik:
3106 Timanus Lane, Ste. 101; Baltimore, MD 21244
1-800-537-2166

Mill Hill Beads, Gay Bowles Sales:
P.O. Box 1060; Janesville, WI 53547
1-800-356-9438

Zweigart-Joan Toggart Ltd.:
2 Riverview Dr.; Somerset, NJ 08873
www.zweigart.com; email-info@zweigart.com

If you have any questions or comments, please contact:
Chapelle Ltd.
P.O. Box 9252
Ogden, UT 84409

(801) 621-2777
Fax (801) 621-2788
chapelle@chapelleltd.com
www.chapelleltd.com

It is our great pleasure to introduce the first-time stitcher to the exciting world of counted cross-stitch. As designers and teachers of the Kooler Design Studio, Inc., this book is close to all of our hearts.

Our editor, Deanna Hall West, is expertly equipped for the task we have set before her. Her years of teaching, re-searching, and writing are put to excellent use as her love of cross-stitch is evident within these pages.

We all fondly remember our first exposure to counted cross-stitch or recall the precious memory of a handmade gift passed down from generation to generation. We hope you experience this joy after easily mastering the beginning techniques. Then you'll be ready to advance into more complicated designs in Section 3. The final section is a gallery where the designers have an opportunity to display their favorite and most advanced work.

We hope that we inspire, educate, and support all who wish to enter the wonderful world of counted cross-stitch. Enjoy!

Donna Kooler

Table of Contents

Cross-Stitch for the First Time

Introduction

Almost every culture has used cross-stitch to embellish clothing as well as religious and household items. Cross-stitch is one of the oldest, yet one of the simplest embroidery stitches, and counted cross-stitch is one of the oldest and simplest embroidery techniques. Counted cross-stitch is worked on an even-weave fabric—a special type of fabric, which has the same number of woven vertical and horizontal threads per inch. You, the stitcher, will count these fabric threads to form each stitch and to know where to place the next stitch.

Cross-Stitch for the First Time is an easy-to-use reference book that has the counted cross-stitch beginner in mind. It compiles the basic information about this stitching technique into a logical step-by-step format. The information includes what fabrics, flosses, and tools to use, how to cross-stitch on different types of materials, different kinds of stitches, and builds upon that basic knowledge.

Each technique emphasizes a particular aspect of cross-stitching—from stitching on Aida or linen, to stitching with fractional stitches. Other techniques include stitching on various foundation materials, stitching with beads, and personalizing each stitched piece. Each technique builds upon what you learned in the previous techniques. The designs themselves are delightful, but not so large or complicated as to daunt a cross-stitch beginner. You will find the instructions are thorough and easy to follow.

The following pages are meant to inspire, gently educate, and thoroughly guide the beginning stitcher into the wonderful world of counted cross-stitch.

How to Use this Book

For the person who is trying cross-stitching for the first time, this book provides a comprehensive guide to supplies and techniques that can be used to create beautiful cross-stitched pieces.

Section 1 familiarizes you with the basic tools, supplies, and general techniques you need to begin cross-stitching.

Section 2 begins with the most basic technique—how to do counted cross-stitch on Aida fabric and takes you to stitching on linen, gradually adding more complex stitches and techniques.

Section 3 takes you beyond the basics, introducing you to more advanced cross-stitching techniques and designs.

Section 4 provides a gallery of ideas and cross-stitched designs by artists and professionals in the field.

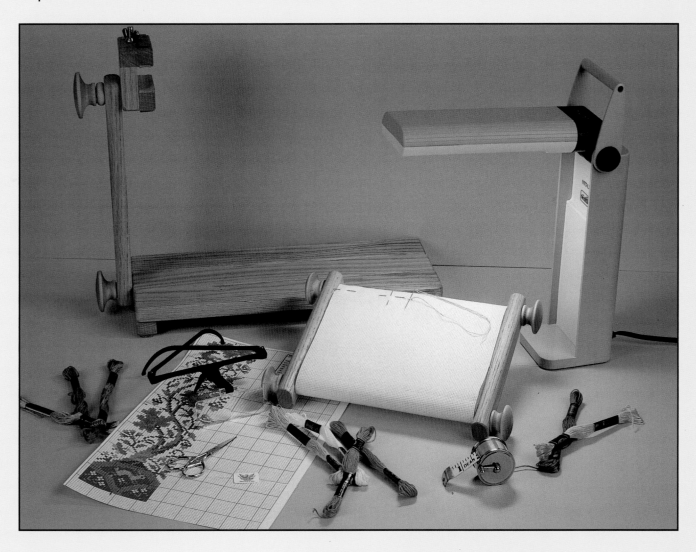

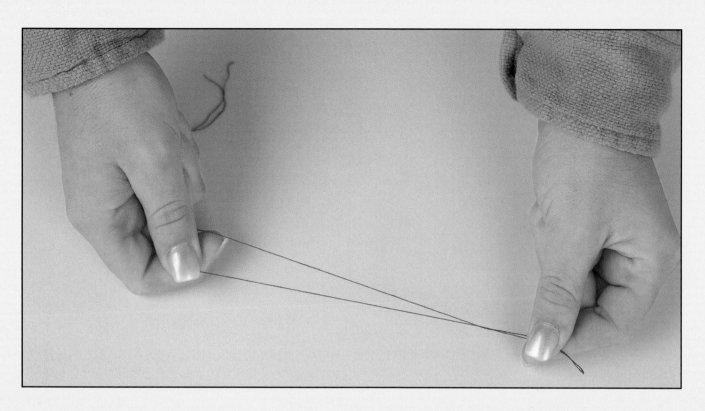

Section 1: *cross-stitching basics*

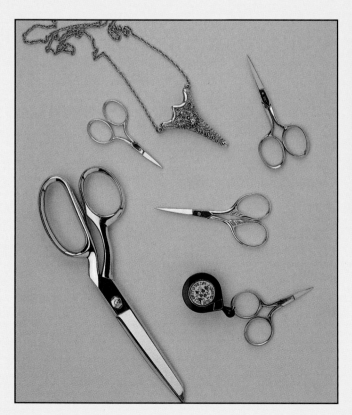

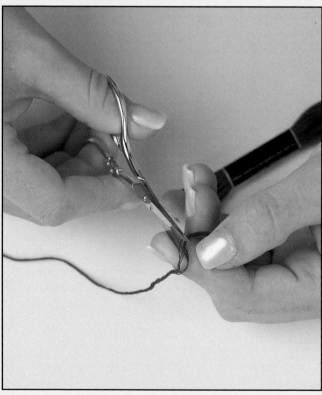

What Do I Need to Get Started?

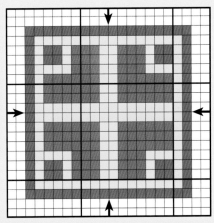
Graph showing colored squares.

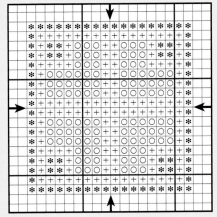
Graph showing symbols.

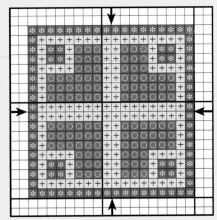
Graph with centering arrows, colored squares, symbols, and key at right.

DMC Floss	
XS	
745	⊞
3328	◉
562	✳

Note: "XS" means cross-stitch.

Graphed Designs

• Cross-stitch designs are graphed on a gridded background. Each square on the graph represents a single cross-stitch.

• Graphs usually have one or two extra grid rows surrounding the design.

• Bold lines occur every ten grid squares.

• Arrows indicate the center of the graph.

• The stitch count for the width of the design is expressed first, then the height.

• Each symbol, colored square, or combination of these elements on the design represents a single cross-stitch in a particular floss color.

• The key to the symbols is adjacent to the graph and indicates which floss color and brand to use for each stitch.

Fabrics

Cross-stitch is worked on an even-weave fabric, which means that the same number of threads are woven horizontally (weft) as vertically (warp). This assures that the same number of cross-stitches will be created in each direction of the fabric and that each individual cross-stitch is square and the same size as the others. Even-weave fabrics come in a variety of thread counts, weave patterns, colors, and fiber content.

Two of the most common even-weave fabrics are Aida (left) and linen (right).

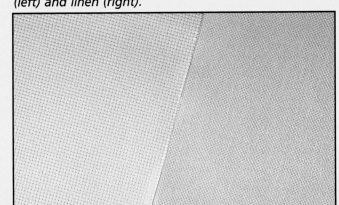

The thread count refers to the number of threads along one horizontal or vertical inch of the fabric for plain-weave fabrics, such as linen. For complex-weave fabrics, such as Aida or Hardanger, the count per inch is determined by squares created in the weave. The thread count in an even-weave fabric determines the size of the design. The higher the number per inch, the smaller the design will be.

The most common even-weave fabrics are cotton Aida, linen, cotton and rayon plain-weave fabrics, plastic canvas, vinyl Aida, and perforated paper. The latter three items are not fabrics but foundation materials upon which cross-stitch can be worked.

Aida: This fabric is the most popular cross-stitch fabric for beginners. This cotton fabric is woven in a complex weave of groups of four threads, which form distinctive small squares with easily visible corner holes.

An individual cross-stitch is formed from corner to corner over each small fabric square. The stitch count of Aida fabrics is based on the number of these squares per inch. Aida fabric is available in 11, 14, 16, and 18 count.

Linen: This is a plain-weave fabric made from flax. Plain-weave means that each fabric thread is woven in the typical over-under method. Normally each cross-stitch is formed over an intersection of two of these fabric threads in both directions (horizontally and vertically). There are no obviously visible corner holes, so it takes a little more practice to learn to cross-stitch on linen.

Linen fabric comes in a variety of thread counts and colors. The most common linen thread counts are 25, 28, 32, and 36 threads per inch. Because the cross-stitches are formed over two threads of the linen, the stitch count is half the thread count. Therefore, if you are using 28-count fabric, then 14 cross-stitches can be formed on one inch of fabric ($28 \div 2 = 14$).

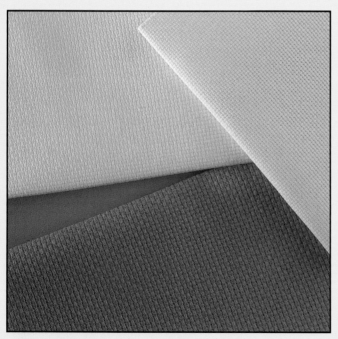

Shown clockwise from top left are 14, 16, and 11 count Aida.

Shown clockwise from top left are linen 25, 36, 28, and 32 threads per inch.

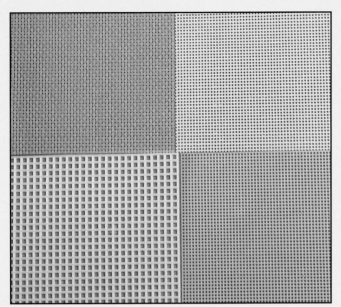

Shown clockwise from top left are vinyl Aida, perforated plastic, perforated paper, and plastic canvas.

Plastic Canvas and Perforated Plastic: Plastic canvas is needlepoint canvas made from plastic and has large square holes. It is available in 8½" x 11" sheets, in three mesh sizes (7, 10, and 14), and in several colors. However, stitchers normally use only the smallest mesh because floss covers this size of grid well.

Perforated plastic has smaller, punched out, round holes. It is available only in 14-count and in 8¼" x 11" sheets. Both plastic canvas and perforated plastic are nonraveling and somewhat rigid. They can be cut for flat holiday ornaments as well as used for three-dimensional items such as boxes, baskets, and ornaments.

Vinyl Aida: More flexible than plastic canvas, vinyl Aida resembles cotton Aida in appearance. It is available in 14- and 18-counts and in seven colors. Vinyl Aida is sold in sheets of several sizes and by the yard. Because vinyl Aida will not rip, ravel, or tear easily, it can be cut to follow any design shape. This product is commonly used for flat items, such as place mats, coasters, and holiday ornaments, as well as dimensional items which are more rounded than those of plastic canvas.

Perforated Paper: This material has been used as a stitching surface for over a century and is still used today. It is available in 9" x 12" sheets and in several colors, but presently only in 14-count. Perforated paper is more fragile than the previous two products. This is used for holiday ornaments, bookmarks, and gift tags.

Needles

Cross-stitch is done with a tapestry needle, which is characterized by a large eye and a blunt tip. This type of needle will slip between the threads and not pierce them.

The size of the needle to use is determined by

Needle threaders make threading your needle easy and are available in a wide variety of styles.

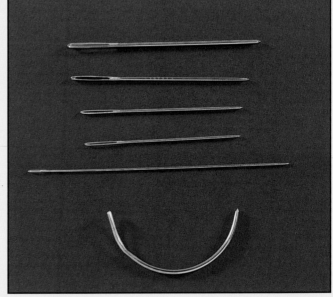

Shown from top to bottom are sizes 22, 24, 26, and 28 tapestry needles, beading needle, and curved tapestry needle.

12

the thread count of the fabric and the number of floss strands to be used. For tapestry needles, the higher the number, the smaller the needle is in length and diameter. Stitchers use size 22, 24, 26, and 28 tapestry needles for most of their work. A size 24 or 26 needle is usually used for cross-stitching on 14-count fabrics.

Because the eye of the needle is made by the needle being struck by a die, one side is more concave than the other. This concave side is easier to thread because the thread is channeled into the hole. If you are having difficulty thread-ing a needle, turn it around and try again. If the difficulty still per-sists, then change to a larger needle or try a needle threader, which is available in several styles.

Use a small emery bag, traditionally shaped like a strawberry, to clean needles. Push the needle into the bag several times. However, if the needle is bent, discol-ored, or rough, throw it away, for damaged needles are difficult to stitch with and may discolor the fabric.

Embroidery Flosses and Threads
Cotton Floss: This is the most commonly used floss for cross-stitch

because of its vast color range, low cost, sheen, availability, and divisible nature. It is available in skeins of six-ply thread, which can be grouped into different numbers of plies as needed (see Fabric, Floss & Needle Chart below). There are several brands available. DMC brand floss colors will be indicated in each graph key.

Fabric, Floss & Needle Chart

Fabric	# of Cotton Floss Strands	# of Silk Floss Strands	Tapestry Needle Sizes
Aida 11	3–4		22–24
Linen 25-ct.	3		24
Aida 14 or Linen 28-ct.	2–3	2	24–26
Aida 16 or Linen 32-ct.	2	1	26
Aida 18 or Linen 36-ct.	2	1	26–28

Shown clockwise from top left are metallics, rayon floss, Danish flower thread, cotton floss, blending filaments, overdyed floss, and silk floss (center).

Silk Floss: This floss is similar to cotton floss, except that it is made of 100% spun silk and is commonly available in either six- or seven-ply skeins. Silk floss has a luxurious sheen, is also divisible, and can be used similarly to cotton floss. However, it is slightly thicker in diameter than cotton floss.

Flower Thread: This thread is made from cotton, has a fine twist, and comes in a matte finish. Flower thread was originally designed to be used as a single thread on 14-count fabrics. It is slightly thicker in diameter than a single strand of cotton floss. Flower thread is not divisible like cotton floss, so you will use it as it comes from the skein. One strand of flower thread equals two strands of cotton floss.

Rayon Thread: This thread is 100% rayon (viscose), available in four- or six-ply skeins, and extremely shiny. This thread is tricky to control, but by slightly moistening it with a barely damp, clean sponge you can straighten out any kinks and better control it.

Overdyed Cotton or Silk Floss: These flosses, regardless of fiber content, are irregularly dyed with several colors or several hues of the same color family. Manufacturers of these overdyed flosses create many different color combinations in both bold and subtle gradations. The changeable color patterns create a dramatic effect without the stitcher having to constantly change floss color in the needle. In order to avoid creating a tweedy effect, stitch each cross-stitch individually before proceeding to the next.

Metallics: Metal "threads" may be added to needlework for additional elegance and glitz. The earliest real metal threads were difficult to work with because of their stiff and fragile nature. Now softer, more pliable, synthetic metallic threads are available in many weights and textures. Because they are made from acetate or a similar product, they are easier to work with and require less care, yet they add the same texture, dimension, and luster as the early real metal threads did.

The most popular of today's metallics are marketed as metallic embroidery threads and flosses, blending filaments, braids, ribbons, cords, and cables.

Blending filament is a one-ply metallic thread, which can be used alone or in combination with other threads to add sparkle to water, snow, stars, feathers, and flowers. Braids and ribbons of various sizes may be used alone for a more textured metallic look. Cord is a one-ply, tightly twisted metallic thread, which can be used for outlining. Cable is a three-ply, heavy, metallic thread used for special effects.

Scissors

Embroidery Scissors: A pair of small, sharp-pointed scissors is a "must-have" accessory. They

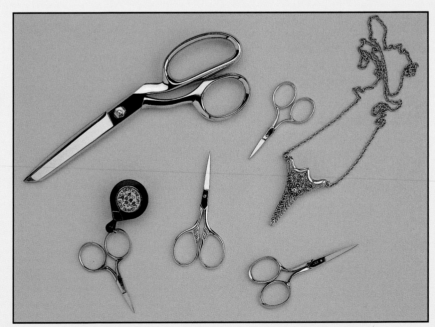

Fabric scissors (top left) and embroidery scissors are a must for cross-stitching. Embroidery scissors come in a wide variety of styles.

are used not only for cutting lengths of floss, but also come in handy for cutting out misplaced stitches and for trimming the floss ends on the back of the stitched fabric.

Fabric Scissors: A pair of 8"-long shears is necessary for cutting the even-weave fabric.

Craft Scissors: Use a pair of craft scissors when cutting plastic or paper canvas.

Measuring Tools

Tape Measure: A flexible tape measure is useful for measuring dimensions longer than 18" and around curved items.

Ruler: Straightedged rulers of several lengths are a necessity. Plastic see-through rulers of 1" x 6" and 2" x 18" lengths are generally the most useful for cross-stitch projects. For measurements longer than 18" use a tape measure or a yardstick.

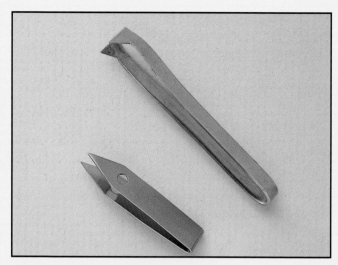

Shown above are two popular styles of tweezers especially designed for cross-stitching.

behind on the fabric where stitches once resided, and to remove pet hair from stitched pieces.

Fabric-stretching Devices

Although cross-stitch can be worked with the fabric held only in the hands, many stitchers find that fabric-stretching devices are ideal for keeping the stitch size and tension consistent, and the design fabric clean. Remember to add an extra inch or two to the total fabric size for this stapling or tacking process.

Wooden Stretcher Bars: Special wooden stretcher bars are made exclusively for needlework. They are narrower and weigh less than the stretcher bars traditionally used for painting canvas. Needlework stretcher bars range in length from 4" to 40" and are easy to use.

Note: For design fabrics less than 8" in width and length, use miniature stretcher bars. They are smaller and weigh even less than the traditional needlework stretcher bars.

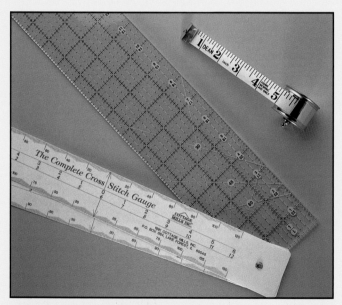

Rulers and tape measures are useful in cross-stitching. A transparent ruler is highly practical because it allows you to see the stitching under it.

Tweezers

Needlework tweezers are available in several sizes and shapes. They are used to help pick out unwanted stitches, to remove tiny fibers left

After you assemble the stretcher bars, attach the design fabric to the wooden frame, using brass tacks or lightweight ¼" staples. You will eventually cut away the margin of the design fabric where you placed the tacks, or staples, so rusting need not be a concern. To prevent raveling of the fabric edges, use 1"-wide drafting or masking tape to hold the fabric onto the stretcher bars.

Plastic Stretcher Frames: These frames are available in 6", 8", 11", and 17" lengths. They are lightweight, interchangeable, and easy to use. The design fabric is rolled around the outside of a PVC frame and held in place with clips that are almost the same length as each frame side. To tighten the fabric almost drum-tight, roll the clips toward the back of the frame.

Wooden Scroll Frames: Scroll frames have been used for hundreds of years. They consist of short wooden sidebars in which you insert wooden dowels at the top and bottom. These dowels can be purchased in various lengths to fit many projects. The design fabric is attached to these two dowels, usually by hand-sewing the fabric to twill tape which has been stapled to the dowels. Turn the dowels to stretch, loosen, or simply move the working area of the design fabric. This type of frame is especially good for long pieces of design fabric, such as bellpulls.

Hoops: These stretchers are made from wood, plastic, or metal rings and usually range in size from 3"–14" in diameter. Use a hoop with the screw-type tension adjuster for best results.

When stretching fabric in a hoop, be certain to keep the horizontal and vertical grain of the fabric straight within the hoop. Because hoops distort the fabric at point of contact, be certain to release the hoop rings at the end of the stitching period. Avoid placing the hoop rings over preexisting stitches, for it realigns and smashes them. Use a hoop that surrounds the design completely or use a different type of fabric stretcher.

Stands

Adjustable lap and floor stands are available to hold hoops, scroll frames, and stretcher frames and bars. These allow the stitcher to stitch more quickly by using both hands, to be

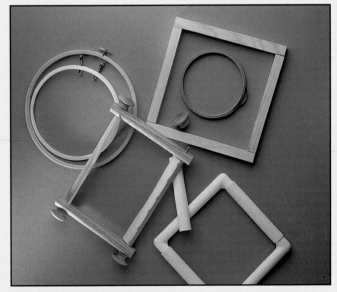

Show clockwise from top left are hoops, wooden stretcher bar, plastic stretcher, and wooden scroll frames.

Floor stands help reduce fatigue and free your hands for ease in stitching.

Lap stands may also be used on a tabletop, and are portable.

more comfortable while stitching, and to maintain optimal posture.

Floss Holders and Organizers

Palettes: These are designed for flosses and are available in flat shapes (rectangles, butterflies, ovals) of wood, card stock, or plastic with a series of holes near the edges. Attach the cut lengths of floss through the holes with a larks-head knot. This keeps the floss lengths sorted by color, instead of in a jumbled pile. Palettes are most useful when working with the precut flosses that come with kits.

Plastic Storage Bags: Specially sized zip-close plastic bags are available for storing individual skeins, reels, or bobbins of embroidery floss. These bags have a corner hole and an area for identifying color, number, size, and brand of the floss within. You can conveniently store the flosses for a project in these bags, organized on a binder ring. After a project is finished, the leftover strands can once again be stored with other flosses in separate bags in a box awaiting the next project.

Paper Envelopes: The simplest and most cost-effective method of conveniently storing different flosses is to place them in small paper envelopes (size 6) with the contents label written in an upper corner. You can store these envelopes in a cardboard shoe box (large sneaker boxes are ideal).

Clockwise from top left are plastic storage bags, straight edge palette, butterfly palette, and paper envelopes.

Light Sources

Usually, we are not aware that our homes do not provide sufficient illumination for easy stitching until we experience eyestrain. You can solve this problem easily by moving a floor or table lamp close to your stitching chair. If this still does not provide enough light, especially in the evenings, take heart, many solutions are available.

Neck Lights: There are many different portable light models which hang from the neck and provide illumination directly onto the stitching surface. The one drawback to these neck lights is that they can feel somewhat heavy after wearing them awhile.

Table and Floor Stand Lights: These usually have more wattage and are better light sources than neck lights, but they are often too heavy to carry

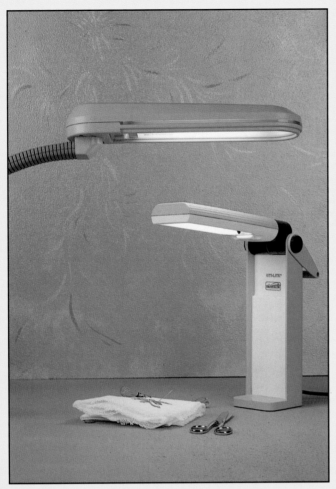

Table lights and floor stand lights are brighter than neck lights and help to ease eye strain when stitching.

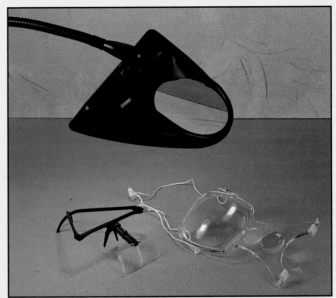

Clockwise from top left are floor light with magnifier, neck light with magnifier, and magnifying glasses.

to a friend's home or to class. There are plenty of lightweight, easy-to-assemble table models. It is a good idea to tuck an extension cord in with your light, in case you end up sitting too far from a plug.

Magnification

Unfortunately, not all of us have perfect eyesight for needlework. Some need a little help to thread the needle and to see those small fabric holes. The solution is magnifiers, which may hang a-round your neck, fit upon your head, be worn on your glasses, or set on tables. Some even have built-in light sources. Make certain when purchasing magnifiers that the optics do not distort the images.

Pincushion or Needle Book

A pincushion is a handy accessory to have near when stitching and a ready place to store threaded needles, extra needles of various sizes, and pins. Pincushions come in a multitude of sizes, shapes, and styles, and, of course, you can make your own.

A needle book is a small fabric book containing "pages" in which to store needles and pins. A needle book is a good idea in households with small children or pets because the sharp pins and needles are stored safely out of sight.

Place Keepers

Place keepers are simple devices that help a stitcher to maintain their stitching place on the graph or to mark the spot where one stops stitching. Sticky notes make simple place keepers. More elaborate place keepers are strips of see-through colored plastic, which are held onto the page by static electricity, or brightly colored rectangles with clear see-through windows of plastic, which attach to the graph by repositionable adhesive.

Drafting or Masking Tape

Drafting or masking tape binds the fabric edges to prevent raveling or to hold the fabric edges onto a stretcher bar frame.

Determining the Amount of Fabric Needed

Each grid square on the graph is equal to one stitch. Included with most graphs is a statement of the precise size (stitch count) of the design (not the graph).

Stitch Count: 25w x 22h

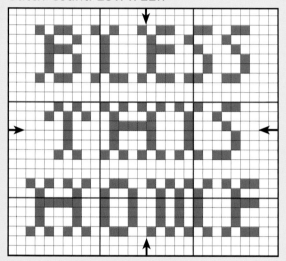

Note: This information saves the stitcher from having to count the grid squares along each axis. However, if this information is lacking, simply count the number of squares that the design (not the graph) encompasses horizontally and vertically.

The design size information may also be accompanied by a short list of three or four of the most common fabric counts (number of stitches per inch) and the size in inches of the design on those particular fabric counts (see Fabric Count Chart above). When this information is not provided, then calculate the size of the design for the intended fabric.

To determine the finished size of the design for a particular fabric, divide the number of grid

---

Fabric Count Chart

Stitch Count: 70w x 126h
Design Size:
Aida 14 or 28-ct. linen	5" x 9"
Aida 16 or 32-ct. linen	4⅜" x 7⅞"
Aida 18 or 36-ct. linen	3⅞" x 7"

---

squares (stitch count) by the stitch count of the chosen fabric.

Example 1:
Stitch Count: 70w x 126h
Fabric: Aida 14 (stitch count is 14 stitches per inch)
Width: 70 ÷ 14 = 5" width
Height: 126 ÷ 14 = 9" height

Fabric: 28-count linen (thread count is 28, but the stitch count is 14 because two threads are used for each cross-stitch)
Width: 70 ÷ 14 = 5" width
Height: 126 ÷ 14 = 9" height

Example 2:
Stitch Count: 70w x 85h
Fabric: 32-count linen (thread count is 32, but the stitch count is 16 because two threads are used for each cross-stitch)
Width: 70 ÷ 16 = 4.38" (~4⅜") width
Height: 85 ÷ 16 = 5.3" (~5¼") height

Add a minimum of 6" to each dimension after you determine the design size before cutting the fabric to allow for finishing. However, if you want to place the design off-center on the finished project or you desire more fabric around the design for any reason, then consider these factors before cutting the fabric.

Design Size: 5"w x 9"h
Cut fabric: 11"w x 15"h
   (5"w + 6" fabric allowance = 11"w; 9"h + 6" fabric allowance = 15"h)

Determining the Number of Floss Strands to Use

Use the number of strands indicated for the design. If this information is not included or if your chosen fabric is not the same as the model, then use the Floss Strand Chart as a guide to determine the number of floss strands to use for the cross-stitches, backstitches, and French knots.

Floss Strand Chart

Stitch Count	# of Floss Strands to Use		
	Cross-stitch	Backstitch	French knot
11	3–4	2	2
14	2–3	1	1–2
16	2	1	1
18	2	1	1

Preparing the Floss

1. Pull an 18" length of floss from the skein.

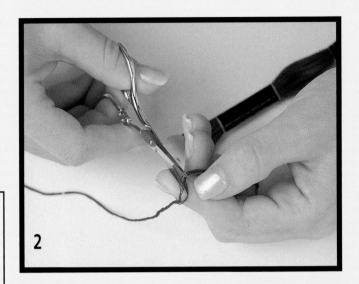

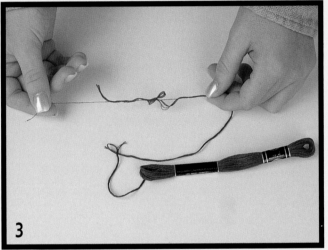

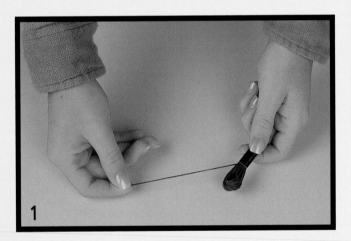

up ends. Then repeat this procedure until you have pulled out the number of floss strands needed for the design. Leave the remaining cut strands with the rest of the skein.

Notes: This procedure removes the artificial twisting of the floss when it was wound into the skein at the manufacturing plant.

Plying floss gives a fuller and smoother appearance to the stitches.

2. Cut through 3–5 strands, 18" from cut end.

Note: This procedure keeps cut strands of floss with numbered skein.

3. To ply or strip the floss, hold cut end in left hand (right if you are left-handed) and remove a single strand of floss by pulling straight out. Stroke or shake out the curled-

4. Align all the cut strands of floss as they come from the skein, with the newly cut ends at the same end.

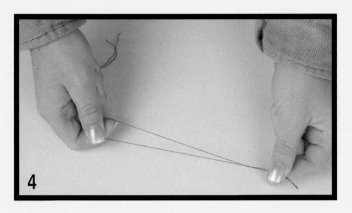

4

Securing the Floss Ends to Begin Stitching

There are four main methods of securing your floss ends. Try each one and select the one you like best. Avoid using permanent knots to begin or end the stitching.

Method #1 - In-line Waste Knot: Knot one end of the floss and insert the threaded needle from the front to the back of the fabric about 1" to the right of where the first line of stitches will fall. Bring the needle back to the front of the fabric where you want to place the first stitch, pull the floss so that no slack is left on the back, and begin stitching. After you have made several stitches over the floss on the back of the fabric, cut the floss tail close to the fabric.

Note: Diagrams of stitches and steps are often used in place of photography.

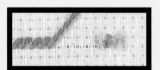

Front view

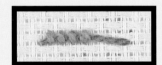

Back view

Method #2 - Away Waste Knot: Knot one end of the floss and insert the threaded needle from the front to the back of the fabric about 3" to the upper left of where the first stitch starts. Bring the needle back to the front of the fabric where you want to place the first stitch, pull the floss so that no slack is left on the back, and begin

stitching. Complete the stitching with this color of floss. On the wrong side of the fabric, cut away the knot, rethread the needle with this newly cut end, and secure the end under the stitching.

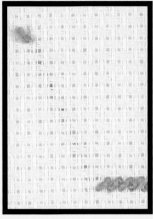

Front view   *Back view*

Method #3 - Standard: With a finger, hold the floss ends on the back of the fabric under the row where you will begin your first few stitches. As you stitch, the floss ends will be caught and held securely between the fabric and the stitches. After four to six stitches, turn the fabric to the back and trim the ends close to the fabric surface. This procedure takes some flipping back and forth to make certain that all of the ends are caught in the stitches.

Method #4 - Thread Loop: Cut a length of floss

Front view

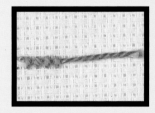

Back view

about 36" (twice as long as normal), place the cut ends together, and thread both cut ends through the needle. Bring the needle to the front of the fabric, where the first stitch starts (be careful not to pull the thread loop through the fabric). Stitch

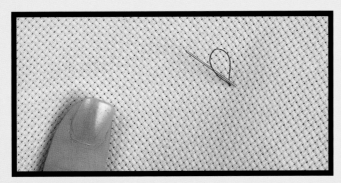

Put needle through thread loop.

the first half of the cross-stitch, put the needle through the thread loop formed on the back, "snug up" the stitch, and continue with the next stitch. This method works only when you are using an even number of floss strands—one long length for two strands, two long lengths for four strands, three long lengths for six strands.

Preparing the Fabric for Stitching

1. Press the fabric.

2. Finish the raw edges of the design fabric to prevent raveling. Machine-zigzag, serge, whipstitch, or overcast by hand, apply drafting or masking tape or fray preventative.

Note: You will cut away these finished edges after the design is stitched.

3. Determine where to start stitching on the fabric, using one of two methods.

Method #1: Find the center of the design by drawing horizontal and vertical lines from the centering arrows through the center of the graph. If a design does not have centering arrows, find the outermost stitches of the design, then count the number of squares horizontally (stitch count of the design only) and divide by two to find the midpoint. Repeat this procedure to find the midpoint for the vertical direction. Remember most graphs will have one or two extra rows beyond the design itself, so avoid including these squares in your stitch count.

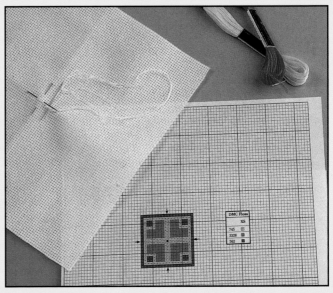

The center of the graph corresponds to the center of the fabric.

Find the center of the fabric by folding the fabric in half and then in half again. Mark the center point of the fabric with a pin or small thread tack.

Method #2: Determine the design size for the specific fabric chosen. Measure 3" down from the top of the fabric and 3" in from the left side of the fabric. Remember that you added a total of 6" to both dimensions to determine the cut size of the fabric. This allows for 3" per side of extra fabric beyond the design itself. This method is particularly useful when stitching long narrow designs like band samplers or bellpulls.

4. Center and stretch the fabric into a stretching device and begin stitching. Remove any pins or thread tacks (avoid stitching over them).

Removing Stitching Errors

Frequently check and recheck to make certain your stitch placement is correct, because counting errors are inevitable. It is less annoying to "unstitch" a few stitches rather than many. As a general rule, avoid reusing floss that has been previously stitched. Remove this worn floss and start fresh with new floss. If you need to remove only two or three stitches, then you can probably reuse this floss.

If, unfortunately, you need to remove many stitches, then it is best to carefully clip the top leg of each errant cross-stitch on all but the last ten stitches or so. Unstitch the last ten stitches in order to leave a long enough tail (no less than 2") to end the thread easily.

To remove the bits of thread fibers remaining in the fabric (especially visible dark threads), use tweezers for the larger thread pieces. To remove the last of the thread fibers, daub both the front and back of the fabric with the adhesive side of transparent tape.

Ending the Stitching

When about 2" are left of the working thread, or when you are finished with thread color for that area of the graph, secure and cut the end of the thread.

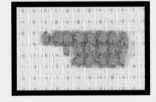

To end the working thread, take a straight stitch through the backs of four or five of the previously worked stitches and trim the thread close to the surface. If the working thread is slippery (rayon thread), then make a return long stitch through the backs of the stitches one row above or below the first straight stitch.

Note: If dark colors are secured under light-colored stitching, the light colors often appear darker or dirty on the front side.

Carrying Threads from One Area to Another

Avoid carrying threads across unstitched areas of the fabric. End the working thread, then begin the stitching again in the new area.

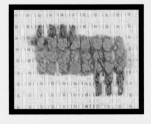

Avoid carrying threads more than 2" on the back of the stitching. If you want to carry the working thread over more than four stitches on the back of the fabric, secure the thread in the back of one or two stitches of the same color or a color of similar value. Do this every third stitch, but avoid carrying the working thread further than a total of about 2" on the back. If you must travel distances more than 2" with the working thread, end the thread, then begin the stitching again in the new area.

Preparing the Design Fabric for Finishing

Note: If the design fabric contains silk threads or overdyed threads, which are not guaranteed colorfast, avoid washing the design fabric. Try to keep it as clean as possible as you stitch.

1. After stitching is completed, hand-wash design fabric in mild soap and water. Place fabric in this solution and gently agitate the fabric occasionally for about five minutes. Avoid scrubbing hard on specific dirt areas, for this will mar the fabric surface or misalign the stitches.

2. Rinse the design fabric thoroughly in several changes of clear water. If the color from the floss bleeds, continue to agitate the fabric in several more changes of the water until all bleeding stops and the water is clear.

3. Roll the design fabric in a clean, dry, white

terry towel and squeeze the roll tightly. Remove as much water as quickly as you can from the design fabric.

4. Unroll the design fabric and lay it face down on another clean, dry, white terry towel. Press the wrong side of the design.

Notes: The towel prevents the stitches from being crushed and cushions any beads during ironing.

When stitching contains silk or metallic threads, use a pressing cloth between the iron and fabric.

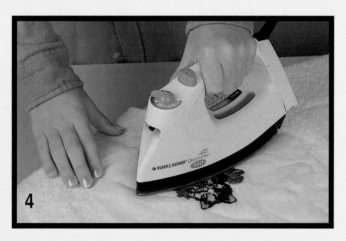

5. Hang the ironed design fabric from a clean plastic clothes hanger, using plastic clips, or

roll onto paper cylinders covered by acid-free tissue paper. Cover the design fabric with more acid-free paper.

Notes: Avoid placing the ironed fabric into a plastic bag because the ironed fabric may not be completely dry yet and mildew may occur.

When transporting the design fabric, you may use a plastic bag temporarily, but avoid storing stitched designs in plastic bags.

Framing a Finished Cross-stitch Design

How you frame your stitching opens up many possibilities and you will have to make a few decisions. What color and style of frame molding do you want? Do you want a single mat or multiple mats? What colors? What finished size do you envision? Do you want the framed piece to coordinate with a certain room color or decor? Do you want glass? This may sound overwhelming, but do not despair; your best friend at this point is a good, reliable, professional framer. Ask your cross-stitching friends or your local needlework shop for a recommendation.

Keep an open mind when choosing a frame. Often another frame color, mat color, or molding style than originally planned turns out to be a better combination. The framer can help guide you to the best possibilities. Then rely on your own judgement, for this is a very subjective decision. If you want glass in the frame, be certain to choose a frame with enough depth to accommodate the spacers needed to keep the glass from touching the stitches.

After you have made all of the framing decisions, you can ask the framer to cut the backing board for you to take home. Most stitchers prefer to lace their design fabric to these boards themselves. This can substantially reduce the cost of framing because lacing is labor-intensive, but in reality fairly simple.

1. Measure the backing board and keep these dimensions handy.

2. Adhere polyester fleece to one side of the backing board with white fabric glue or spray adhesive.

3. Trim the fleece. Cover the fleece with a washed piece of cotton fabric that matches the color of the design fabric.

4. Pull the fabric snug so there are no wrinkles and adhere the raw edges to the back of the board. Set aside.

5. Center the design. With light-colored sewing thread, sew a running-stitch box around the design the same dimensions as the backing board. Make certain these running stitches maintain the same spacing between threads from corner to corner. If you do not intend to center the design within the frame, make the necessary adjustments.

6. Trim the design fabric 1½" beyond running stitch lines. Zigzag or overcast-stitch raw edges. Align the running-stitch lines with the top and bottom of the backing board and pin the design fabric to the edge of the backing board. Start at the center top and bottom and work outward alternately to the corners, pinning every ½" or less. Design fabric should be taut. Repeat this pinning sequence for the sides.

7. Check to make certain the design fabric is sufficiently taut. If it is not, make adjustments now. Move pins several threads toward the design on all sides. Repeat until you are satisfied the fabric is taut enough.

8. Using needle and heavy home decor thread or dental floss, lace the design fabric to the backing board. Lace the larger dimension first, starting in the middle, and lace to within 1½" of corners. Repeat for other dimension. Miter corners and stitch down.

Note: Your prepared design fabric is now ready to take back to the framer or to insert into the frame, with or without mats.

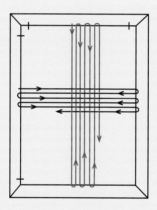

9. Use small brads or glazier points to lightly tack the design unit into the frame.

10. Cover the back of the frame with brown paper or decorative wrapping paper.

11. Attach a picture hanger or wire to the frame back.

6

Section 2: *stitching basics*

How Do I Cross-stitch on Aida Fabric?

What You Need to Get Started:

Aida
Floss as indicated on
graph

———————

Shown stitched on
white Aida 6

Stitch Count:
25w x 22h

Design Size:
Aida 6 - 4¼" x 3⅝"
Aida 11 - 2¼" x 2"
Aida 14 - 1¾" x 1⅝"
Aida 18 - 1⅜" x 1¼"
Linen 32 over 2 -
    1½" x 1⅜"

Aida fabric is a good fabric on which to begin cross-stitching. There are several things to keep in mind when beginning your first design. Remember that the lower the number of threads per inch, Aida 14 for example, the larger the stitch. Stitch one cross-stitch over every square on Aida fabric.

Bless This House

Here's How:
Use the small open corner holes in the fabric to place the two legs of each cross-stitch. Stitch one cross-stitch for every colored and/or symboled square on the graph.

There are two basic methods of stitching cross-stitches. Regardless of which method you use, let your needle dangle frequently from the fabric to allow the thread to untwist and to reduce knotting.

Method #1—Horizontal Stitches:
1. Work from left to right in a horizontal row. From back of fabric, come up at 1 and go down at 2. Come up at 3 and go down at 4, continuing across the row until you have the required number of stitches.

2. Come up at 5 and go down at 6. Come up at 7 and go down at 8, continuing

until you have crossed all of the half-cross stitches to form complete cross-stitches.

Note: Avoid mixing this example of forming cross-stitches with the following example because the top stitch of this cross-stitch is formed from lower right to upper left, rather than from lower left to upper right.

Method #1—Reverse Horizontal Stitches:
1. You can also work from right to left in a horizontal row. From back of fabric, come up at 1 and go down at 2. Come up at 3 and go down at 4, continuing across the row until you have the required number of stitches.

2. Come up at 5 and go down at 6. Come up at 7 and go down at 8, continuing until you have crossed all of the half-cross stitches to form complete cross-stitches.

Method #1—Vertical Stitches:

1. From back of fabric, come up at 1 and go down at 2. Come up at 3 and go down at 4, continuing vertically until you have the required number of stitches.

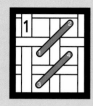

2. Come up at 5 and go down at 6. Come up at 7 and go down at 8, continuing until you have crossed all of the half-cross stitches to form complete cross-stitches.

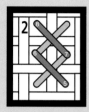

Method #2—Single Stitches:

1. From back of fabric, come up at 1 and go down at 2, then come up at 3 and go down at 4, completing each cross-stitch before going onto the next cross-stitch in the row.

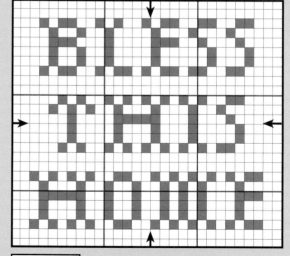

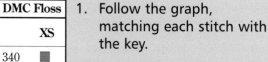

DMC Floss	
XS	
340	■

1. Follow the graph, matching each stitch with the key.

The left piece was stitched with pearl cotton thread and the right with six strands of floss.

Note: This method uses slightly more thread because of the diagonal stitch, which carries from one stitch to another on the back of the fabric.

Railroad Technique:

Use this technique whenever you are using two strands of thread for stitching, to keep these strands parallel (like railroad tracks) for the best coverage and the nicest looking stitch.

1. When completing your stitch, go down into hole between two thread strands; pull your thread through the hole to the back to complete the leg of the stitch.

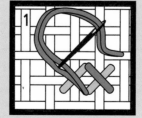

2
technique

How Do I Cross-stitch with More Than One Color of Floss?

Most cross-stitching pieces use more than one color of floss to add details and create motifs. Each symbol on the stitch diagram is color-coded to a floss color.

What You Need to Get Started:

Aida
Floss as indicated on graph

Shown stitched on white Aida 14

Stitch Count:
18w x 18h

Design Size:
Aida 11 - 1⅝" x 1⅝"
Aida 14 - 1¼" x 1¼"
Aida 18 - 1" x 1"
Linen 32 over 2 -
    1⅛" x 1⅛"

Four-heart Quilt Block

Here's How:
1. Follow the graph, matching each stitch with the key.

DMC Floss	
XS	
745	+
3328	◉
562	✳

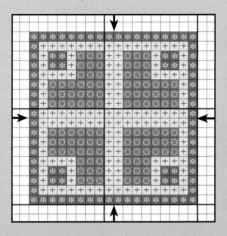

How Do I Backstitch?

Use the backstitch to outline motifs, for lettering, and for accents such as eyelashes, whiskers, fold lines, and other fine detail.

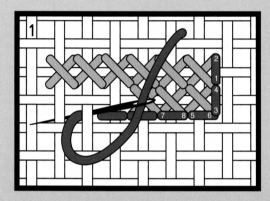

Welcome

Here's How:

1. From back of fabric, come up at 1, go down at 2, come up at 3, go down at 4, come up at 5, and go down at 6, continuing with the forward-two-stitches, back-one-stitch pattern.

What You Need to Get Started:

Aida
Floss as indicated on graph

Shown stitched on white Aida 14

Stitch Count:
68w x 56h

Design Size:
Aida 11 - 6⅛" x 5⅛"
Aida 14 - 4⅞" x 4"
Aida 18 - 3¾" x 3⅛"
Linen 32 over 2 -
    4¼" x 3½"

DMC Floss		DMC Floss		DMC Floss		
XS		**XS**		**XS**		**BS**
White	⋅	350	▣	826	N	⌐
746	−	304	M	955	S	
745	○	209	+	912	E	
743	%	208	⁙	561	★	
783	H	3761	◇	869	♥	
352	△	3766	✳			

Note: "BS" means backstitch.

Backstitching Diagram only

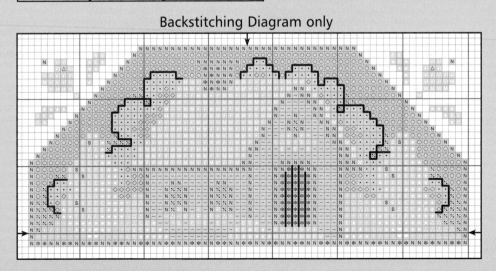

How Do I Cross-stitch on Linen and Other Plain-weave Fabrics?

To cross-stitch on linen fabric, stitch one cross-stitch over every two threads horizontally and vertically. Stitch one cross-stitch for every colored or symboled square on the graph. Cross all top stitches in the same direction.

What You Need to Get Started:

Floss as indicated on graph
Linen

Shown stitched on white Cashel linen 28

Stitch Count:
69w x 81h

Design Size:
Aida 11 - 6¼" x 7⅜"
Aida 14 - 4⅞" x 5¾"
Aida 18 - 3⅞" x 4½"
Linen 32 over 2 - 4¼" x 5"

33

Flower Cat

Here's How:

There are two methods of cross-stitching on linen:

Method #1—Horizontal Stitches:

1. Work from left to right in a horizontal row. From back of fabric, come up at 1 and go down at 2, covering two 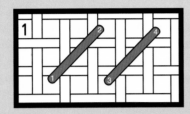 threads vertically and two threads horizontally. For accuracy, count both horizontally and vertically rather than diagonally. Come up at 3 and go down at 4, continuing across the row until you have the required number of stitches.

2. Come up at 5 and go down at 6. Come up at 7 and go down at 8, continuing until you have crossed all of the 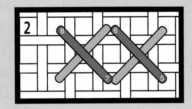 half-cross stitches to form complete cross-stitches.

Note: Avoid mixing this example of forming cross-stitches with the following example because the top stitch of this cross-stitch is formed from lower right to upper left, rather than from lower left to upper right.

Method #1—Reverse Horizontal Stitches:

1. You can also work from right to left in a horizontal row. From back of fabric, come up at 1 and go down at 2, covering two threads vertically and two threads horizontally. Come up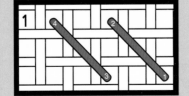

at 3 and go down at 4, continuing across the row until you have the required number of stitches.

2. Come up at 5 and go down at 6. Come up at 7 and go down at 8, continuing until you have crossed all of the half-cross stitches to form complete cross-stitches.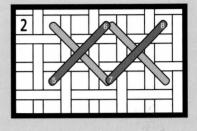

Method #1—Vertical Stitches:

1. From back of fabric, come up at 1 and go down at 2, covering two threads vertically and two threads horizontally. Come up at 3 and go down at 4, continuing vertically until you have the required number of stitches.

2. Come up at 5 and go down at 6. Come up at 7 and go down at 8, continuing until you have crossed all of the half-cross stitches to form complete cross-stitches.

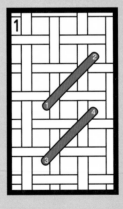 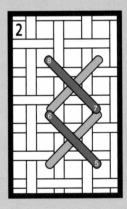

Method #2—Single Stitches:

1. From back of fabric, come up at 1 and go down at 2, covering two threads vertically and two threads horizontally. Come up at 3 and go down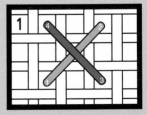

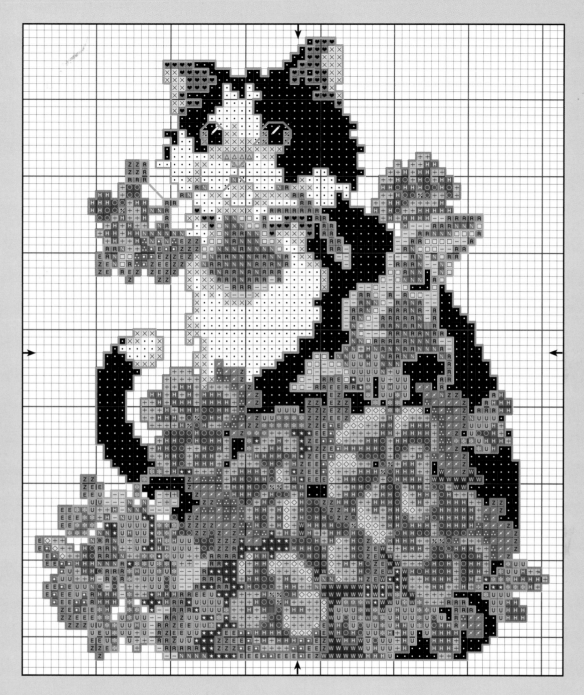

at 4, completing each cross-stitch before
going onto the next cross-stitch in the row.

*Note: This method uses slightly more thread be-
cause of the diagonal stitch, which carries from
one stitch to another on the back of the fabric.*

DMC Floss			DMC Floss			DMC Floss		
	XS	**BS**		**XS**	**BS**		**XS**	**BS**
White	·	⌐	304	◉		3348	−	
3820	▨		814	W	⌐	989	R	
963	◇		917	◨		987	N	
760	△		209	◪		986	★	⌐
893	+		552	⬖		3072	✕	
3608	Z		959	U		648	♥	
3805	E		3814	✳		310	■	⌐
349	H		772	▢				

35

5
technique

How Do I Read a Split Graph?

36

What You Need to Get Started:

Aida
Floss as indicated on graph

Shown stitched on ivory Aida 14

Stitch Count:
32w x 140h

Design Size:
Aida 11 - 3" x 12¾"
Aida 14 - 2¼" x 10"
Aida 18 - 1¾" x 7¾"
Linen 32 over 2 - 2" x 8¾"

Many graphs are too large to fit on a single page of a book or leaflet and must be split into two or more parts. A graph may be divided horizontally, vertically, or both.

Tree of Life

Here's How:
A graph may be divided singly or into many parts. The bold lines that occur every ten grid squares help in reassembling the graph parts. You can tape full-sized color photocopies of the sections together, matching the design at the grid lines, to aid in finding the correct place to continue stitching.

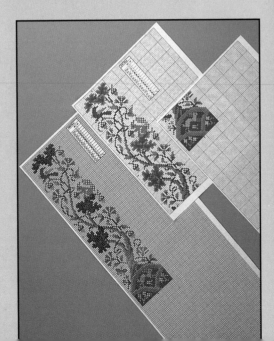

Top

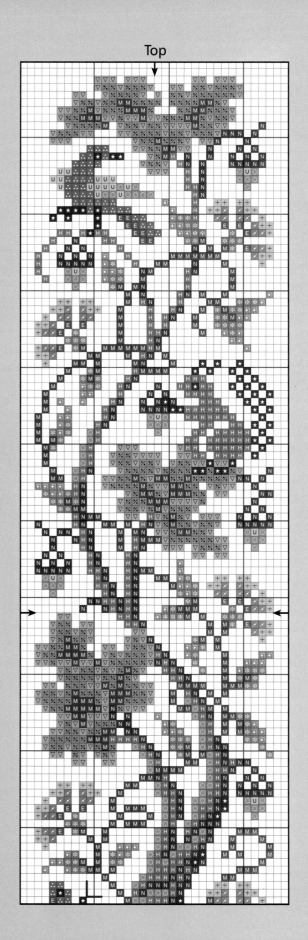

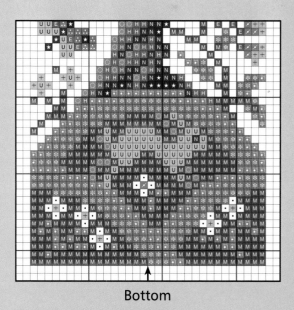

Bottom

DMC Floss		
	XS	**BS**
White	·	
676	U	
3609	+	
209	◿	
208	E	
340	⬚	
3013	▽	
471	◩	
988	✳	
502	▨	
561	M	
3828	◯	
434	H	
801	N	
3371	★	⌐

How Do I Stitch Specialty Stitches?

Although the cross-stitch and the backstitch are the predominately used stitches in counted cross-stitch, other stitches will create special effects. You will often find the following specialty stitches in cross-stitch designs.

What You Need to Get Started:

Floss as indicated on graph
Linen

Shown stitched on ivory Cashel linen 28

Stitch Count:
48w x 104h

Design Size:
Aida 11 - 4⅜" x 9½"
Aida 14 - 3⅜" x 7⅜"
Aida 18 - 2⅝" x 5¾"
Linen 32 over 2 - 3" x 6½"

One Good Turn

Here's How:
Stitch these stitches in the same manner regardless of whether you are using Aida or linen.

French Knot (FK)
A French knot is a small, knotted stitch that is most often represented by a small dot on the graph. Place one or two tight wraps of the working thread around the needle before taking the needle to the back of the fabric. Avoid using the same hole from which the thread emerged. Using the same hole often pulls the small knot through the fabric to the back. The size of the knot is determined by the number of strands of threads in the needle, not the number of wraps of thread around the needle. The more wraps, the more lopsided and less spherical the knot will be.

1. From back of fabric, come up at 1, twist the thread around the needle once or twice, snug the wraps around the needle.

2. Go down at 2.

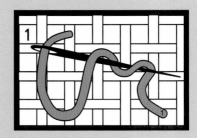

Long Stitch (LS)
A long stitch (also called a straight stitch) is a single straight stitch that is longer than the length of one normal stitch on the fabric. In other words, it is longer than one fabric square on Aida and longer than two threads on linen. A long, straight line on the graph often represents the long stitch. This stitch looks different than a normal backstitch. A long stitch may also disregard the formed holes of Aida and the normal backstitch placement on linen.

1. From back of fabric, come up at 1 and go down at 2.

Note: If using more than one strand of thread, make certain that the strands remain parallel and untwisted (see Railroad Technique on page 29).

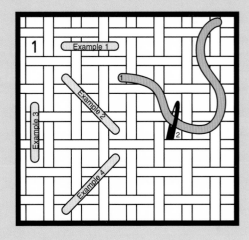

Couched Line (CT)
Sometimes a long stitch is so lengthy that an extra stitch or two is needed to keep it in place, to keep it from being snagged, or simply for decorative purposes. When this occurs, it is called a couched line or couching.

1. From back of fabric, come up at 1, go down at 2, come up at 3, go down at 4, come up at 5, go down at 6, continuing the length of the long stitch.

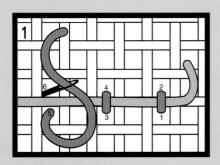

Lazy Daisy (LD)
The lazy daisy is a single, detached chain stitch, and is one of the most popular of all embroidery stitches. It is often represented by a teardrop outline on the graph.

1. From back of fabric, come up at 1 and go down at 2 (which may be the same hole as 1 or immediately adjacent to 1). Leave a small loop of thread on the surface of the fabric. Come up at 3, placing the loop of thread under the point of the needle.

2. Loosely snug the thread loop up to the work-

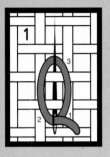

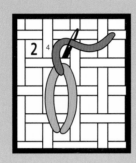

ing thread. Go down at 4, tacking the thread loop in place.

Upright Cross-stitch (UX)

An upright cross-stitch is done the same as a regular cross-stitch, except it is oriented like a + sign, rather than an X.

1. Come up at 1, go down at 2, come up at 3, and go down at 4.

Smyrna Cross (SX)

A Smyrna Cross stitch consists of a full cross-stitch with an upright cross-stitch on top. It is usually represented by a double cross-stitch symbol on the graph.

1. From back of fabric, come up at 1, go down at 2, come up at 3, and go down at 4, forming a cross-stitch.

2. Come up at 5, go down at 6, come up at 7, go down at 8, forming a double cross-stitch.

DMC Floss								
	XS	BS	FK	LS	LD	SX	CT	UX
3064	▫					▦		
3722	▪		●			▦		
597	✳		●			▦		
3813	△							
3815	H							
3052	✚				○		✕	
422	◿					▦		
3828	◎							
420	N					✳		
610	★	⌐	●	╱	○	▦		✛

Top

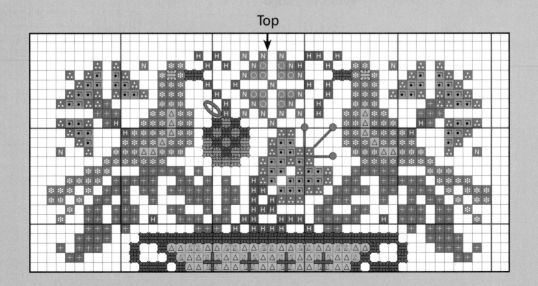

Bottom

Floss as indicated on
    graph
Linen

Shown stitched on
    cream Cashel
    linen 28

Stitch Count:
48w x 83h

Design Size:
Aida 11 - 4⅜" x 7½"
Aida 14 - 3⅜" x 5⅞"
Aida 18 - 2⅝" x 4⅝"
Linen 32 over 2 -
    3" x 5¼"

How Do I Stitch Fractional Cross-stitches?

Fractional cross-stitches are partial stitches that do not cover the entire small fabric square on Aida or cover the normal 2 x 2 threads on linen or other plain-weave fabrics. Cross-stitch designers use them to help achieve smoother, rounder, more natural shapes.

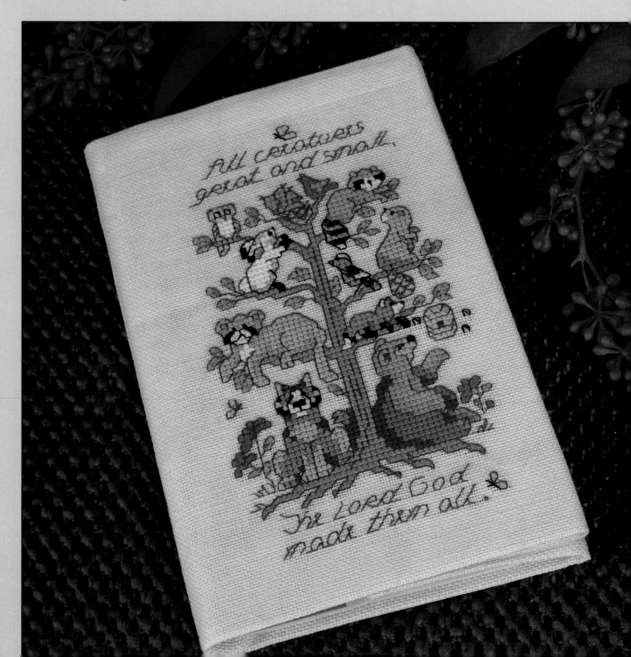

Animal Tree

Here's How:
There are two types of fractional cross-stitches:

Note: These illustrations show fractional stitches as they would appear on linen.

Quarter stitch
Quarter stitches may occupy any of the corners into the center. Therefore, quarter stitches can begin from four different directions: upper left, lower left, upper right, and lower right.

1. Stitch a quarter stitch (half leg of a half-cross stitch). From back of fabric, come up at 1 and go down at 2.

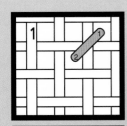

Three-quarter stitch
1. From back of fabric, come up at 1 and go down at 2, stitching a quarter stitch for the first leg. Come up at 3 and go down at 4, stitching a half-cross stitch for the remaining leg.

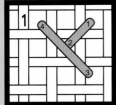

How Do I Stitch Opposing Fractional Cross-stitches?
In graph squares where there are opposing fractional cross-stitches, you have three options:

Option 1:
1. Stitch each as a quarter stitch when a backstitch divides them.

Option 2:
1. Stitch each as a three-quarter stitch.

Note: If a backstitch divides them, stitch the backstitch between the two long legs of the two three-quarter stitches.

Option 3:
1. Stitch one of the fractional cross-stitches as a quarter stitch and another as a three-quarter stitch.

Note: This latter situation requires you to make a decision as to which stitch is dominant (three-quarter stitch).

Fractional Cross-stitches on Aida and Linen
Creating fractional cross-stitches on Aida is slightly more difficult than on linen. The necessary center hole for the quarter stitch is not formed in the small fabric squares. You must create this hole by pushing the blunt tapestry needle into the center of the four inner fabric threads.

Creating fractional cross-stitches on linen or other plain-weave fabrics is easier than on Aida because these fabrics already have the necessary center hole, formed by the weave of the fabric.

DMC Floss				
	XS	**BS**	**FK**	**LS**
White	·			
676	◎			
352	+			
350	▣			
932	▨			
368	◇			
3814		⌐	●	
738	U			
3064	E			
402	△			
922	N			
301	★			
300	✳	⌐		╲
842	⊟			
841	▨			
839	M			
310	▪	⌐	●	

How Do I Stitch Using Two Thread Colors or Two Different Threads in a Single Needle?

Combining two different floss colors in a single needle is referred to as a tweeded or blended needle. There are several reasons for this technique. It softens the color transition between two floss colors, produces a floss shade not available, or produces a definite tweedy or bicolor effect.

What You Need to Get Started:

Aida
Floss as indicated on graph

Shown stitched on white Aida 14

Stitch Count:
25w x 27h

Design Size:
Aida 11 - 2¼" x 2½"
Aida 14 - 1¾" x 1⅞"
Aida 18 - 1⅜" x 1½"
Linen 32 over 2 -
   1½" x 1¾"

Carnation

Here's How:

Using Two Floss Colors in a Single Needle:

Color transitions may be between two shades of the same color, such as periwinkle and blue, or two different colors of similar value, such as a medium orange and a medium yellow.

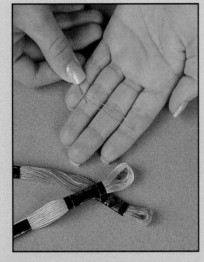

The tweedy effect uses dissimilar colors, such as black and beige or blue and yellow.

Using Metallic Threads

Wonderful and exciting embroidery threads are available, which can add constantly changing color (overdyed floss), subtle sparkle (metallic blending filaments), elegance (gold, silver, and copper metals), or even fluorescence (glow-in-the-dark threads) to your stitching. These specialty threads vary in size, usage, and flexibility, and are available in many colors. Some can be used in combination with your floss, while others are stitched singly.

Metallic and metal embroidery threads have different meanings. Metallic means those threads which appear to be made from metal but are actually made from synthetic materials, while metal is applied to those threads which have a large amount of real metal (gold or silver) in them.

Hint: To cut metallic threads, use a separate pair of scissors or use the area of the blades closest to the handles of your embroidery scissors. This latter method keeps the front portion and tips of the scissor blades sharp for cotton or silk threads.

Using Blending Filaments

Blending filaments are thin, one-ply, soft metallic threads, which come in over 65 colors and four color styles (basic, high luster, glow-in-the-dark, and vintage). All of these filaments produce a shine or glow to your stitches. The high-luster type produces the most shine.

Usually you combine one or two shades of these metallic filaments with your floss in the same needle but you can use them without the floss. Most frequently, you add a single strand of blending filament to your floss strands; but if you want to add two strands for more glimmer, then you need to reduce the number of floss strands by one.

Hints when stitching with blending filaments:
• Use 18" (or shorter) lengths of all thread in the same needle.

• Knot the blending filament(s) onto your needle when combined with floss or used alone.

• Stitch more slowly to achieve better control of the blending filaments.

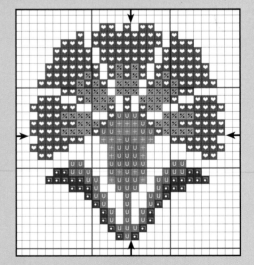

DMC Floss	
XS	
776 3733	⊠
335 3731	♥
3348	+
3346	U
986	◨

Note: Brackets indicate a blended thread.

How Do I Stitch Using Specialty Threads?

Additional metallic threads, overdyed floss, and rayon threads are other specialty threads that can add beauty and detail to your stitched pieces.

What You Need to Get Started:

Floss as indicated on graph
Linen

Shown stitched on white Cashel linen 28

Stitch Count:
40w x 102h

Design Size:
Aida 11 - 3⅝" x 9¼"
Aida 14 - 2⅞" x 7¼"
Aida 18 - 2¼" x 5⅝"
Linen 32 over 2 - 2½" x 6⅜"

Grow with Love

Here's How:

Using Other Metallic Threads

This category of metallic threads consists of all other metallic threads, except blending filaments. It is slightly more difficult to stitch with these threads because they are a little stiffer, and separate or fray easily. However, the result of gold or silver accents or overall opalescence is decidedly worth the slight inconvenience.

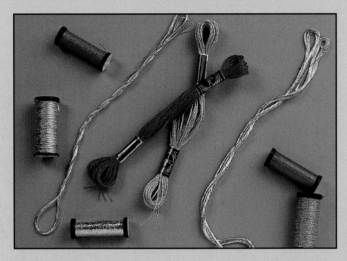

To help control the fraying of these threads, cut short thread lengths (12"–14") and stitch with the needle positioned 2" from one cut end. When the ends begin to separate and fray, end the thread and start a new thread.

Using Overdyed Floss

Overdyed floss consists of cotton threads with a random pattern of several colors or shades of the same color along the thread length. You must complete each cross-stitch individually to allow both legs of the cross-stitch to match and not appear tweedy.

Hint: Avoid using the thread-loop method of starting when using these threads (see page 21).

Hint: Avoid using the thread-loop method of starting when using these threads (see page 21).

Using Rayon Threads

Rayon threads are extremely shiny, synthetic threads which you can use in place of cotton floss. They are available in many colors. Rayon threads must be slightly damp during stitching to keep them under control, for they tend to be somewhat "independent." Run the stitching threads over a clean lightly moistened sponge. These threads should be only slightly damp. Anchor these threads more securely than cotton floss.

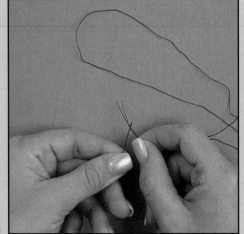

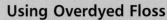

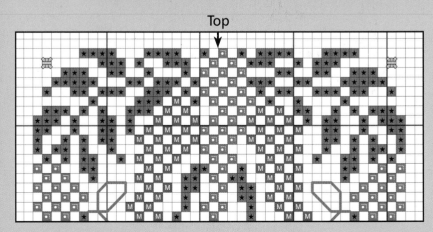

Bottom

DMC Floss						
	XS	BS	FK	LS	SX	UX
White *032BF	⊡					
**180 or DMC 3727	N					
**156 or DMC 315	▦	⌐	●			
**176 or DMC 209	▨					
**178 or DMC 340	M					
**140 or DMC 912	★	⌐				
3828 *002HL	E					
*002HL #4 Braid				╱	▧	✛
*002HL #8 Braid					✳	
*Kreinik Blending Filament & Braids						
**Needle Necessities Overdyed Floss						

49

How Do I Stitch with Beads?

Beads have graced cross-stitch embroidery since before medieval times. Today, we can add glass seed beads to our cross-stitch for added texture, interest, and sparkle.

What You Need to Get Started:

Aida
Floss as indicated on graph

Shown stitched on beige Aida 14

Stitch Count:
50w x 77h

Design Size:
Aida 11 - 4½" x 7"
Aida 14 - 3⅝" x 5½"
Aida 18 - 2¾" x 4¼"
Linen 32 over 2 - 3⅛" x 4¾"

Lone Wolf

Here's How:
The glass seed beads available for cross-stitchers today come in many colors, two sizes (regular, or 11, and petite, or delica), and several finishes (regular, frosted, and antique). The regular-sized seed beads fit the 14- and 16-count fabrics well, while the petite beads are used with 18-count fabrics or for tiny accents.

Stitching Technique
To attach seed beads to the cross-stitch fabric, use a size 28 tapestry needle or a short beading needle. Check to make certain needle size passes through selected size bead hole.

Use one or two strands of floss, depending on what fits through the eye of the bead. In general, choose a color of floss to closely match the bead color. However, sometimes the floss color alters the bead color if it is too dark; in this case choose a lighter floss color.

Use the loop method of threading the needle. With this method, the needle and only two strands of thread pass through the bead, instead of the needle and the usual four strands of thread, used with the conventional method of threading the needle.

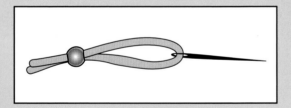

There are two methods to sew seed beads to cross-stitch fabrics. When finished, all beads should be facing the same direction. Both methods attach the bead to fabric in such a manner so that the bead sits upright and does not lay down or flop around.

Method #1:

1. Stitch a normal cross-stitch. From back of fabric, come up at 1, stitch through bead, go down at 2, come up at 3, stitch through bead, and go down at 4.

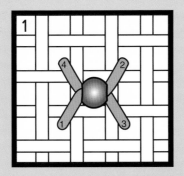

Note: The bead will be oriented vertically.

Method #2:

1. From back of fabric, come up at 1, stitch through bead, go down at 2, come up at 3, and go down at 4, separating floss strands so that one strand lays on each side of bead. Tighten thread tension to hold bead in place.

Note: The bead will be oriented diagonally.

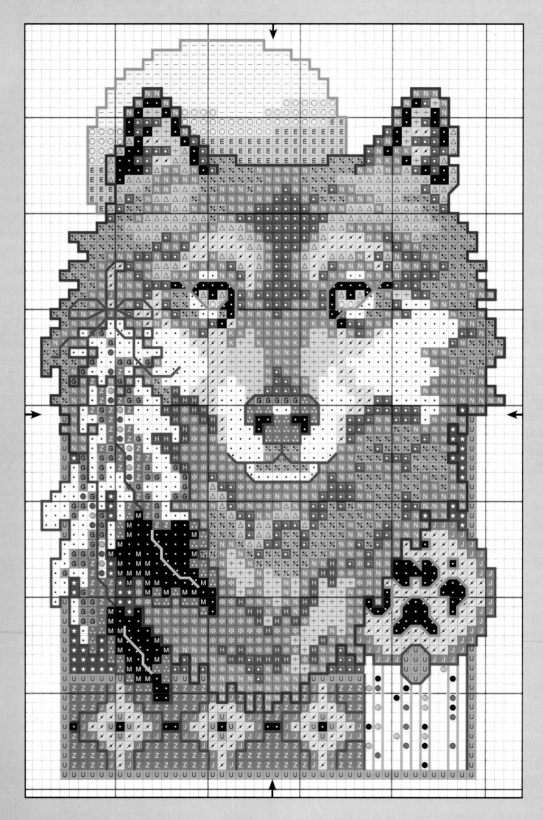

DMC Floss			
	XS	**BS**	**BD**
White	·		
3823	–		
745	○		
676	E	⌐	
951	∕		
350	J	⌐	
209	Z		
208	★		
3766	U	⌐	
437	+		
436	△		
435	K	⌐	
3772	✳		
632	H		
842	▨		
841	N		
839	◨	⌐	
415	G		
414	▨		
413	M	⌐	
310	■	⌐	
*02011			○
*02013			●
*02014			●
*Mill Hill Beads			

Note: "BD" means bead.

How Do I Sign My Stitched Design?

Every cross-stitched piece deserves to have a signature in either cross-stitch or backstitch, with the stitcher's name or initials and the date that the piece was completed.

What You Need to Get Started:

Floss as indicated on graph
Linen

Shown stitched on tea-dyed linen 28

Stitch Count:
61w x 123h

Design Size:
Aida 11 - 4½" x 7"
Aida 14 - 3⅝" x 5½"
Aida 18 - 2¾" x 4¼"
Linen 32 over 2 - 3⅛" x 4¾"

Alphabet Sampler

Here's How:

You can incorporate your initials or name and the date as a definite part of the design, as in the Alphabet Sampler (wrought by...) on page 53, or as a small add-on near the base of the stitched piece. Select a floss color that you have already used within the stitched piece to stitch this information. This provides color continuity between the design and the signature.

Sometimes you may not want to distract in any way from the actual stitched design. In this case, the name and date can be stitched in the same colored thread as the ground fabric, and al-though nearly hidden, the information is still available for future generations.

Choosing Alphabet and Numeral Style and Size

Choose the cross-stitch or backstitch alphabet and numerals that suit the style and size of the stitched piece. A Victorian-style stitched piece warrants an alphabet with more serifs than a geometric piece; a tiny backstitch alphabet is more appropriate for a cross-stitched miniature than a large pictorial piece. However, the style and size of the signature is the stitcher's preference.

Sometimes you may want to use your own logo or personal symbol. Graph this image in several sizes on graph paper and use this personal signature in place of your name wherever appropriate.

A border can also enclose the name and date to further enhance the signature. This is similar to the rectangular border surrounding many Asian signatures (chops). This border can be a simple backstitched rectangle or an elaborate frame.

Some designs have a small area enclosed or partially enclosed specifically for the stitcher's signature. Often this brings up a vexing problem for those stitchers whose initials or name includes wide letters, such as M and W. Occasionally the stitcher has to self-modify these letters to fit within the allotted space or choose an entirely different alphabet which will fit the dimensions.

Placing the Signature

If the design has a special place for the name and date, then use this area. If the design does not have a designated area for the signature, you must decide where to place this information. Often the base or perhaps side of the design is the best

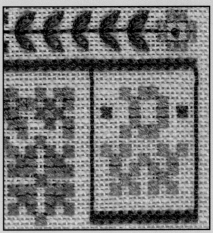

place. However, you can be more adventuresome and place your initials (or name) and the date along branches, on or in leaves, hidden in the grass, or anywhere else that seems appropriate—recorded for posterity but not obvious.

When the fabric will be cut close to the design, for example on ornaments and pillows, stitch the name and date on a separate small piece of

even-weave fabric. Apply this as a patch to the back of the finished piece.

Hint: If the back of the finished piece is an even-weave fabric, the signature may be stitched directly on it.

Gentle Arts Overdyed Floss			
	XS	**BS**	**FK**
Blue Jay or DMC 3807	◼	⌐	●

Top

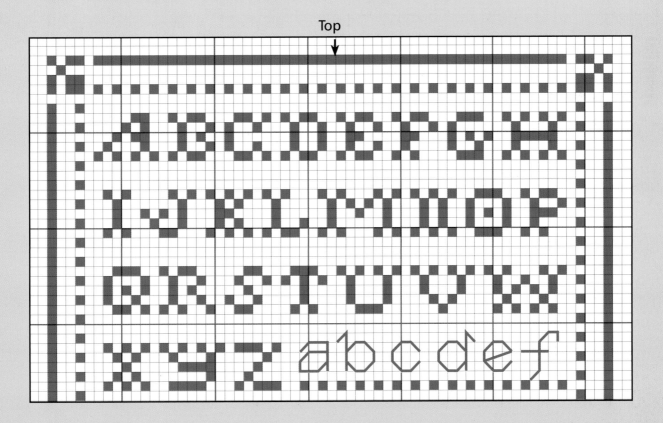

55

Bottom

How Do I Extract a Portion of Design or Extend a Border Design?

Often you can use a graphed design, especially a modular one, for several different projects by simply extracting and stitching whole or partial motifs. One advantage to this procedure is that all of the projects coordinate in color and style.

What You Need to Get Started:

Floss as indicated on
graph
Linen

Shown stitched on
antique white
Cashel linen 28

Stitch Count:
84w x 104h

Design Size:
Aida 11 - 4½" x 7"
Aida 14 - 3⅝" x 5½"
Aida 18 - 2¾" x 4¼"
Linen 32 over 2 -
3⅛" x 4¾"

Bunny Farmers

Here's How:
Extracting a Portion of a Design

Carefully analyze a design to see if there are any separate motifs, which you can simply use to stitch for additional coordinating cross-stitched projects.

If the motifs are complete (no missing parts due to overlapping of design elements), then count the size of the design (width and height). Calculate the motif's size for the even-weave fabric you will use. The count of the fabric determines the stitched size of the motif (see page 19). A good starting point is to calculate the motif size for 14-count even-weave, and then recalculate for other fabric counts if this size is too large or too small for the desired project.

If the desired motif is missing an element or a small portion of the design, then you must either complete the motif (examine the rest of the design for color and shape clues) or eliminate or modify that area. This takes a little more effort and creativity, but usually is not difficult.

In this example, the border from the Bunny Farmers' design was extracted.

Extending a Border Design

Lengthening a border to fit a particular project can be done two basic ways:

Method 1:
1. The simplest method is to choose a complete individual motif and repeat it several times horizontally or vertically, allowing a short distance between each motif.

Method 2:
1. Analyze the motif to see if it has a repeating section and, if so, simply stitch this repeat area again and again until you achieve the desired size.

In this example, the Bunny Farmers are extracted from the original design.

DMC Floss			DMC Floss			DMC Floss			
	XS	BS		XS	BS		XS	BS	FK
White	·		322	Z		3776	S		
745	−		312		⌐	975	⊡		⌐
725	△		563	O		739	⊠		
3609	+		562	H		738	J		
3608	⁘		3348	⅛		842	⊡		
553	E		3347	N		841	G		
3740		⌐	987	⊡		839	✳		⌐
775	✎		895		⌐	310	■	⌐	●
800	◇		402	U					

How Do I Stitch Using Waste Canvas?

What You Need to Get Started:

Floss as indicated on graph
Spray bottle with water
T-shirt
Tweezers
Waste canvas

Shown stitched on T-shirt

Stitch Count:
48w x 104h

Design Size:
Aida 11 - 4⅜" x 9½"
Aida 14 - 3⅜" x 7⅞"
Aida 18 - 2⅝" x 5¾"
Linen 32 over 2 - 3" x 6½"

Waste (also called blue line) canvas is a special, disposable canvas that is held together by water-soluble starch. When you baste this canvas onto almost any noneven-weave fabric, it provides the foundation grid for counted cross-stitch.

Angel

Here's How:

After you stitch the design, you dampen the design fabric and the waste canvas with water, which dissolves the starch holding the canvas together. Using a pair of tweezers, remove the waste canvas thread by thread, leaving the cross-stitched design intact on the noneven-weave fabric. Waste canvas is available in several mesh sizes with the most common being 8½, 10, 12, and 14 squares per inch.

Preparing Waste Canvas for Stitching:

1. Select the design.

Hint: It is easier to remove the waste canvas if the design is not solidly filled in or too large.

2. Choose the mesh size of the waste canvas and calculate the design size (see page 19).

Note: If you want the design to be larger or smaller, then select another mesh size.

3. Cut the waste canvas 2" larger for both dimensions than the calculated design size.

4. Cover the raw edges of the waste canvas with masking tape, drafting tape, or seam binding.

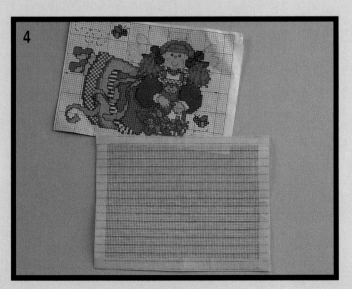

5. Mark the center of the waste canvas with horizontal and vertical running stitches or thread tack.

Stitching on Waste Canvas:

1. Position and baste the waste canvas onto the fabric or clothing item.

Hint: You may baste a lightweight, nonfusible interfacing to the back of lightweight or exceptionally soft fabric to stabilize it, to keep it from puckering or drooping with the weight of the stitching.

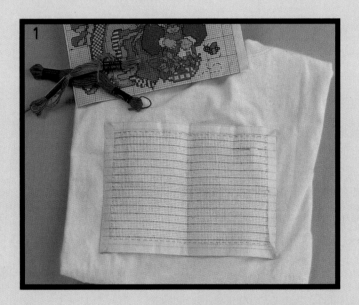

2. Center the design on the waste canvas by matching the center marks. Stitch design, using either a tapestry needle if the fabric is loosely woven or a sharp needle for more tightly woven fabrics.

Note: The trick for successfully stitching on waste canvas is to stitch directly into the center of the holes of the waste canvas, and to stitch somewhat loosely.

3. Trim the waste canvas about ½" from the stitched design.

4. Mist the design and the waste canvas with water.

5. Using tweezers, remove each thread of waste canvas by grasping one end and pulling it out from under the stitching.

Note: Pull slowly and steadily because the threads of the waste canvas are weak and break easily.

6. Press the design fabric.

DMC Floss			DMC Floss			DMC Floss		
	XS	BS		XS	BS		XS	BS
White	·		775	☒		3776	◎	
745	∕		3755	▽		400	⠰	
743	N		826	✳	⌐	977	S	
948	−		312	G		3826	K	
963	+		703	◇		300	★	⌐
962	E		701	H		898		⌐
606	◱		699		⌐	3799	♥	⌐
304	M		402	⁒		*002HL		⌐
347		⌐						
*Kreinik #4 Braid								

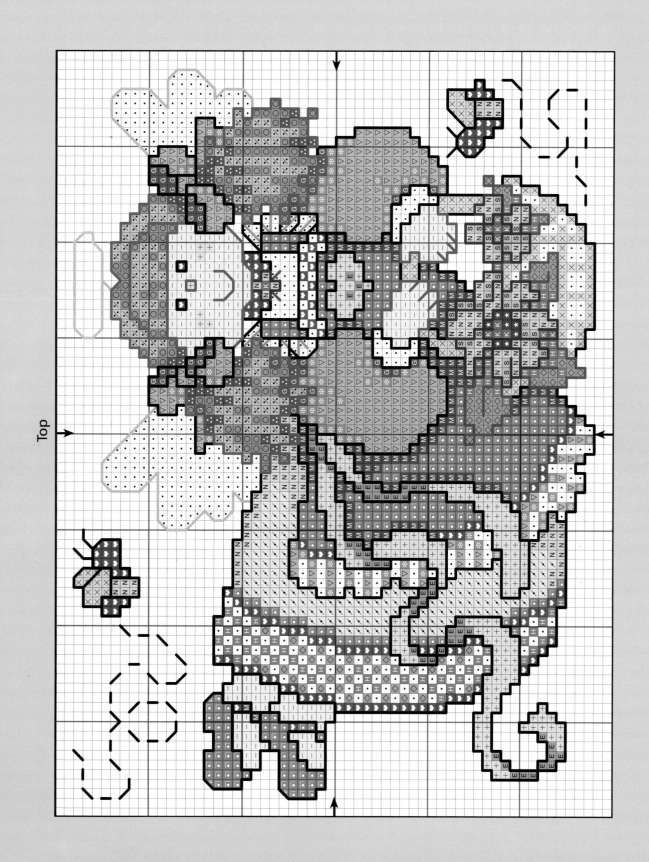

How Do I Stitch on Plastic Canvas, Vinyl Aida, Perforated Plastic, or Perforated Paper?

What You Need to Get Started:

Floss as indicated on graph
Perforated paper; plastic; vinyl aida

**Heart
Stitch Count:
28w x 25h**

Design Size:
Aida 11 - 2½" x 2¼"
Aida 14 - 2" x 1¾"
Aida 18 - 1½" x 1⅜"
Linen 32 over 2 -
    1¾" x 1½"

**Snowman
Stitch Count:
36w x 42h**

Design Size:
Aida 11 - 3¼" x 3⅞"
Aida 14 - 2⅝" x 3"
Aida 18 - 2" x 2⅜"
Linen 32 over 2 -
    2¼" x 2⅝"

**Four Flowers
Stitch Count:
25w x 23h**

Design Size:
Aida 11 - 2¼" x 2⅛"
Aida 14 - 1¾" x 1⅝"
Aida 18 - 1⅜" x 1¼"
Linen 32 over 2 -
    1½" x 1½"

Paper, plastic, and vinyl are fun variations in cross-stitching foundation materials. Although these products resemble the familiar fabric mesh of needlepoint canvas or fabric Aida, they are actually stitching foundations produced in synthetic materials or paper.

Heart on Paper, Snowman on Plastic, and Four Flowers on Vinyl Aida

Here's How:
Paper, plastic, and vinyl do not unravel or need to be blocked or pressed, and the final finishing is simple and easy. Because they are more rigid and hold their shape better than regular cross-stitch fabrics, you can easily create unique three-dimensional or shaped projects.

Avoid using cross-stitch designs containing fractional stitches on these synthetic products because it is too difficult to pierce the plastic or vinyl, and it is not advisable on paper mesh.

You may hand-hold these products or

Plastic canvas, vinyl aida, perforated plastic, and perforated paper may be tacked to a stretcher bar or frame when stitching.

tack them to stretcher bars during stitching. Sometimes the stitching thread gets caught in the rough raw edges. If this is a problem, tape the edges with transparent or masking tape.

Stitch on these synthetic products as you would even-weave fabrics or canvas. Use the smoother side of the sheet for the front of the design.

You can easily cut all of these products to shape. However, wait until all stitching is complete to cut out the shapes. Use a pair of 3"–4" craft scissors dedicated to cutting these synthetic products because they will dull your fabric or embroidery scissors.

Using Plastic Canvas

Molded plastic canvas is available in 7-, 10-, and 14-mesh grid (stitches per inch) sizes. Plastic canvas commonly comes in a clear mesh and is available in rectangular sheets, approximately 11" x 14". Because of its rigidity, plastic canvas is often used for three-dimensional projects (boxes, tissue covers, ornaments), as well as flat items (ornaments, bookmarks).

Four Flowers on vinyl aida

Use a tapestry needle size 16 or 18 for 7-mesh canvas, size 20 or 22 for 10-mesh, and size 24 or 26 for 14-mesh.

Use any thread or yarn as long as it covers the square-shaped mesh completely. Worsted-weight, rug, and craft yarns fit the 7-mesh canvas well; sport-weight, Persian, and tapestry yarns work well on the 10-mesh canvas; and Persian yarn or floss can be used on the 14-mesh canvas.

Using Perforated Plastic Canvas

Perforated plastic canvas (14-mesh grid) has perforated circular holes rather than the vertical and horizontal grid of the other two sizes. Perforated plastic comes in many colors and is available in 8¼" x 11" sheets.

Perforated plastic is more flexible than plastic canvas and is used for projects such as ornaments (flat and three-dimensional) and bookmarks.

Snowman on plastic canvas

Use two or three strands of floss when cross-stitching on 14-mesh and one strand for back-stitch, unless otherwise stated for the design. Specialty threads may be used if they fit the holes. Adjust the number of plies as needed. Cut along the straight lines of the grid or holes of the perforated plastic. Trim any nubs.

Using Vinyl Aida

This 14-count Aida is a synthetic (vinyl) product and has the Aida weave pattern imprinted on it. It is presently available in white, tan, black, and parchment in 12" x 18" sheets or by the yard. It is much more flexible than either plastic canvas or perforated plastic and is suitable for such flat projects as place mats and table runners or for inserts encircling mugs and napkin rings.

Stitch designs on vinyl Aida, using a tapestry needle size 24 or 26. Use 2–3 strands of floss for cross-stitch and one strand for backstitch unless otherwise stated for the design. Specialty threads may be used if they fit the holes; adjust the number of plies as needed.

Vinyl Aida can be cut in any direction. Trim any remaining nubs.

These products may be trimmed to the stitching edge because they will not fray.

Using Perforated Paper

Perforated paper is made from pressed paper with punched-out circular holes in 14 count. It is more fragile than any of the above products, but still rather sturdy. This stitching medium became popular during the Victorian era, and was used for samplers, inspirational framed pieces, valentines, and bookmarks.

Perforated paper is available in several colors besides white and cream, and usually comes in 9" x 12" sheets.

Stitch designs on perforated paper, using a tapestry needle size 24 or 26. Use 2–3 strands of floss for cross-stitch and 1–2 strands for backstitch unless otherwise stated for the design. Specialty threads may be used if they fit the holes. Adjust the number of plies as needed.

Cut perforated paper through the holes. Trim any remaining nubs.

Finishing is easy, but the paper tends to tear if folded or manipulated too much. Perforated paper is especially good for framed pictures and bookmarks.

Heart on perforated paper

Four Flowers

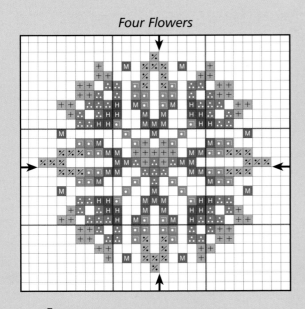

Heart

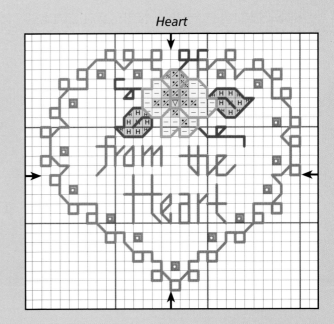

Snowman

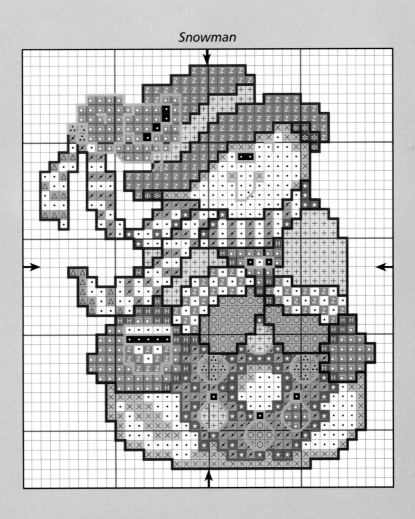

Four Flowers Key

DMC Floss	
	XS
351	+
349	:
815	H
704	%
702	⊡
561	M

Heart Key

DMC Floss		
	XS	**BS**
746	−	
743	▽	
3825	%	
721		⌐
3760	⊡	⌐
3348	H	
699		⌐
434		

Snowman Key

DMC Floss		
	XS	**BS**
White	·	
744	+	
741	:	
3609	O	
606	⊡	
498	H	
3753	×	
799	Z	
797	❋	
959	△	
703	◢	
700	★	⌐
413		⌐
310	▪	⌐

67

Section 3: *beyond the basics*

How Do I Stitch a Design with a Different Color Scheme?

What You Need to Get Started:

Anne cloth afghan
Floss as indicated on graph

Shown stitched on white Anne cloth afghan

Stitch Count:
40w x 40h

Design Size:
Aida 11 - 3⅝" x 3⅝"
Aida 14 - 2⅞" x 2⅞"
Aida 18 - 2¼" x 2¼"
Linen 32 over 2 -
    2½" x 2½"

If you like a cross-stitch design, but would prefer a different color scheme, you may use your own color choices.

DMC Floss								
Orange Motif		Yellow Motif		Pink Motif		Red Motif		
XS	BS	XS	BS	XS	BS	XS	BS	
745 −								
742 ⊙		745		3708		350		
740 ▦		743		3706		666		
606 H		742		3705		817		
817 ▣	⌐	606	⌐	666	⌐	814	⌐	
814 ✦		817		304		310		
3013 +								
3012 %								
3011 M	⌐							
772 ⊠								
989 △								
987 E								
890	⌐							
3827 U								
976 ❋								
3826	⌐							

Green and brown flosses remain the same in all floral motifs.

Nasturtium

Here's How:

In this example, the flower's color scheme changes, but the leaves remain the same. Remember when choosing colors to stay with the same color values, exchanging dark colors for dark and light colors for light.

1. Stitch one design for each color key.

Note: The design shown on page 70 was stitched on a premade afghan.

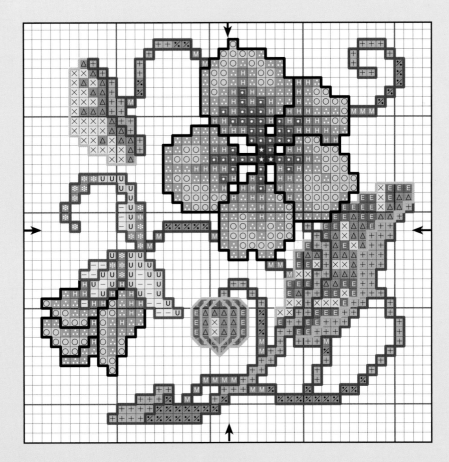

How Do I Stitch Hardanger?

What You Need to Get Started:

Embroidery scissors
Floss as indicated on
   graph
Linen

———◆———

Shown stitched on
   tea-dyed linen 28

Stitch Count:
61w x 123h

Design Size:
Linen 28 over 1 -
   2¾" x 2¾"
Linen 32 over 2 -
   2¼" x 2¼"

Note: Hardanger is worked on linen and is inappropriate for Aida.

Hardanger embroidery originated in Norway and is a technique used on table linens, collars, and cuffs. It is formed by Kloster blocks, which are blocks of five stitches done over four threads.

Traditional Hardanger

Here's How:

Kloster Block (KB)
In this design, Kloster blocks are stitches worked in groups to form squares. After stitching the Kloster blocks, trim away the center that contains no stitching, using sharp embroidery scissors.

1. From back of fabric, come up at 1 and go down at 2. Come up at 3 and go down at 4, continuing for five stitches.

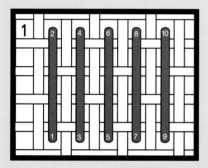

2. When moving from one side of a Kloster block to another, come up at 11, the same hole as 9, and go down at 12, continuing for five stitches. Dashed lines indicate where to cut threads.

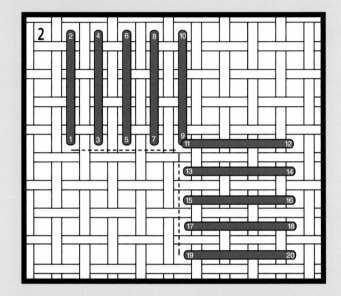

Fagot Stitch (FS)

The fagot stitch is a series of backstitches done in a group that resemble stairs.

1. From back of fabric, come up at 1 and go down at 2. Traveling diagonally from 2, come up at 3 and go down at 4. Traveling diagonally from 4, come up at 5 and go down at 6. Traveling diagonally from 6, come up at 7 and go down at 8. Continue for the required number of stitches.

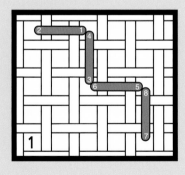

Double Fagot Stitch (DF)

To create a double fagot stitch, forming small squares, simply continue stitching in the reverse direction.

1. To begin the second row for a double fagot stitch, come up at 9, and go down at 10. Traveling diagonally from 10, come up at 11 and go down at 12. Continue stitching the second row until you reach the end of the first row.

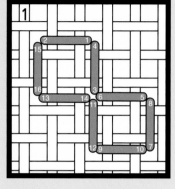

Note: The end of the second row of stitching should come together with the end of the first row, forming a complete square.

Satin Stitch (SS)

1. From back of fabric, come up at 1, go down at 2, forming a straight stitch. Come up at 3, and go down at 4. Continue stitching until area is filled.

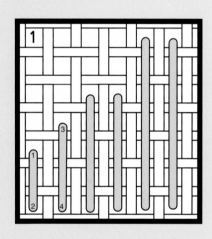

Figure Eight (F8)

This stitch, also known as woven bars, is used between two Kloster blocks to finish the remaining four threads when center threads are cut.

1. From back of fabric, come up at 1 and go down at 2.

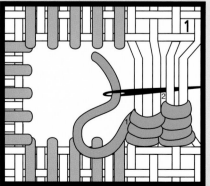

73

2. Come up at 3 and go down at 4. Continue this over-two-under-two pattern until the area is completely filled, but not buckled.

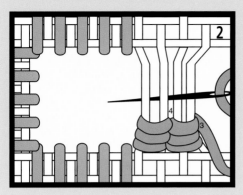

DMC Floss	KB	SS	FS	F8	DF
*Rose Quartz or DMC 3689	‖‖‖	≡			
**Ecru #12			/		//

*Caron Collection Watercolors

**DMC Pearl Cotton

Note: One grid line equals two threads.

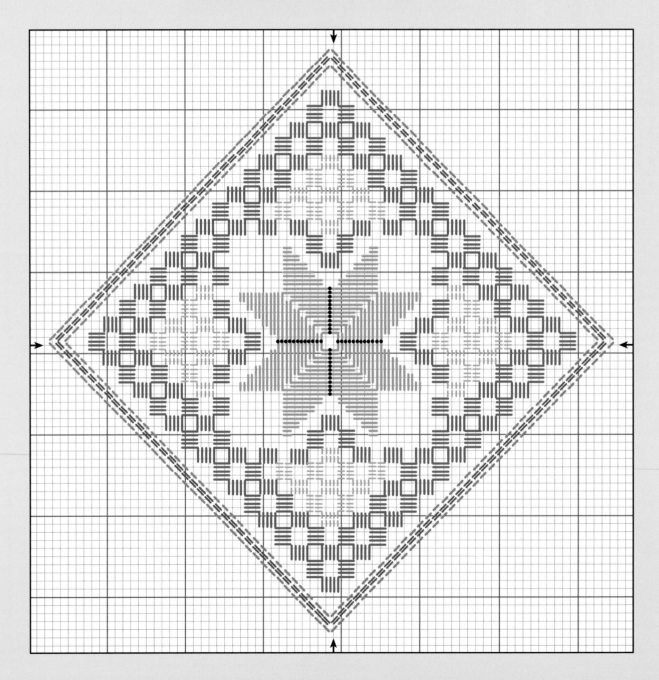

Do I Add Solid Beading and Include Treasures?

...are glass charms and come in a variety of shapes and ...h solid beading and treasures add sparkle and ... a design.

What You Need to Get Started:

Beads as indicated on graph
Floss as indicated on graph
Linen
Treasures as indicated on graph

Shown stitched on tea-dyed linen 28

Stitch Count:
154w x 200h

Design Size:
Aida 11 - 14" x 18¼"
Aida 14 - 11" x 14¼"
Aida 18 - 8½" x 11¼"
Linen 32 over 2 - 9⅝" x 12½"

Wedding Sampler

Here's How:
Add beads and treasures where indicated on graph. See page 51 for instructions on attaching beads.

Bead Loops (BL)
Bead loops add dimension and charm to a stitched piece. Bead loops should be done with a beading needle and a single strand of floss.

1. From back of fabric, come up between woven threads. String number of beads from key onto floss. Go down between same woven threads.

Eyelet Stitch (ES)
1. From back of fabric, come up at 1, between woven threads, and go down at 2. Come up at 3 and go down at 4, the same hole as 2. Continue clock-wise until completed as indicated.

Four-sided Stitch (FSS)
1. From back of fabric, come up at 1 and go down at 2. Traveling diagonally, come up at 3 and go down at 4. Traveling diagonally, come up at 5 and go down at 6. Traveling diagonally, come up at 7 and go down at 8. Continue as indicated.

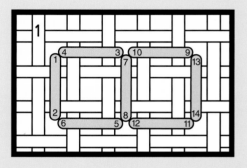

Treasure (TR)
1. From back of fabric, come up between woven threads. String treasure then bead onto floss. Go down into treasure hole and between same woven threads.

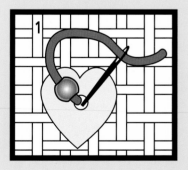

DMC Floss									
	XS	**BS**	**ES**	**FSS**	**FS**	**KB**	**LS**	**BD/ATT W/FLOSS**	**TR/ATT W/FLOSS**	**BL(10)/ATT W/FLOSS**
Ecru			✳	⬜⬜	⬒					
223 ❄										
3752 ▣										
932 (Name)	⌐									
503 Ⓤ										
502	⌐									
739 ▨										
*Ecru #8					▨	/				
**002 ▦										
***3021							+/Ecru		
***3021							○		
***3021									✳/Ecru
***3018							△/Ecru		
***3020							H/Ecru		
***2016							○/502		
***2017							E/932		
***2007							S/Ecru		
***2006							N/Ecru		
****13031								◆/Ecru	
****12086								♡/Ecru	
****12092								♥/Ecru	
****12214								♥/BD3021/Ecru	
****12143								◗/503	
*DMC Pearl Cotton **Kreinik #4 Braid ***Mill Hill Beads ****Mill Hill Treasures									

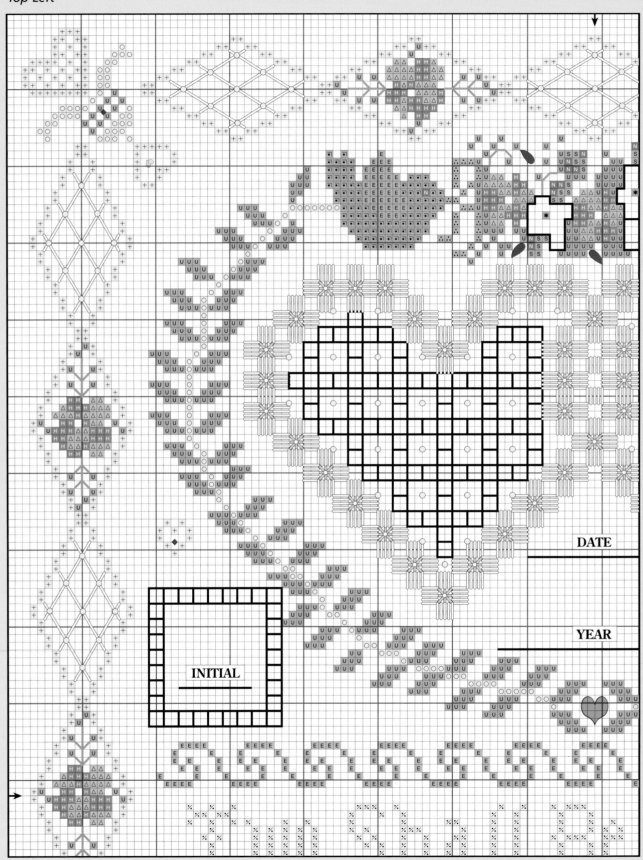

DATE

YEAR

INITIAL

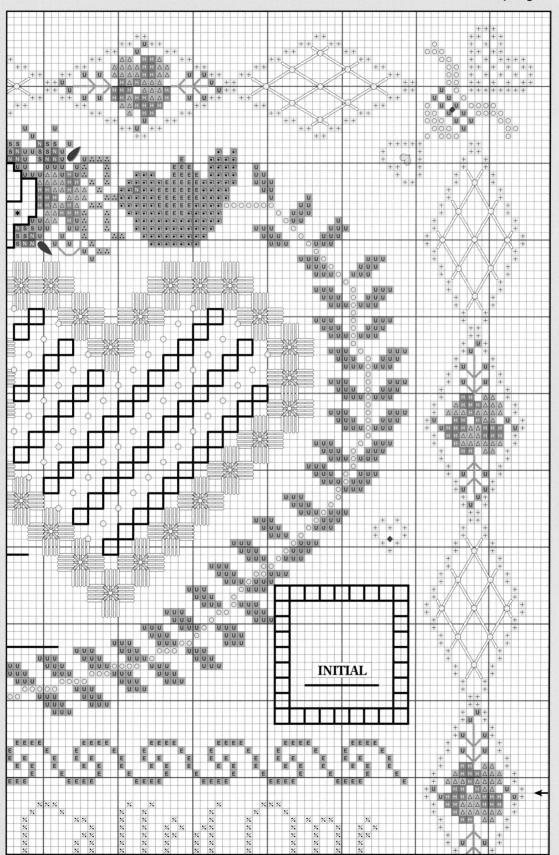

INITIAL

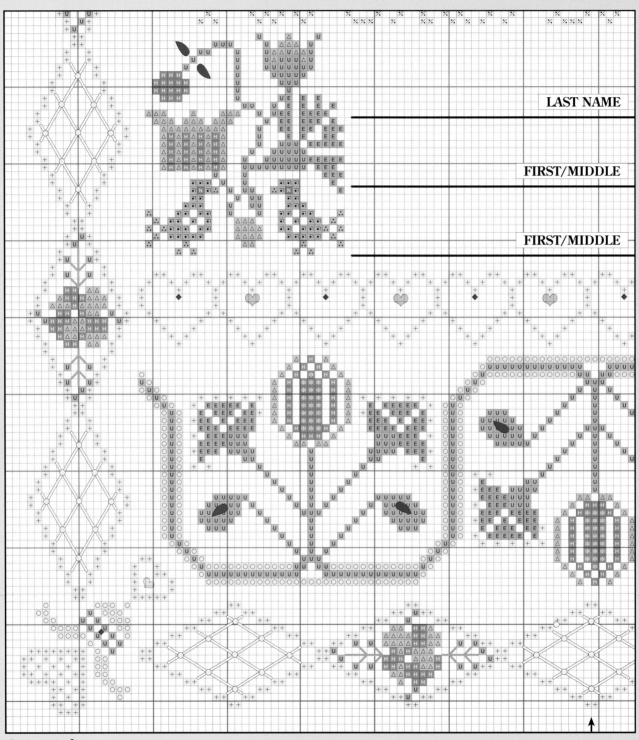

LAST NAME

FIRST/MIDDLE

FIRST/MIDDLE

Bottom Left

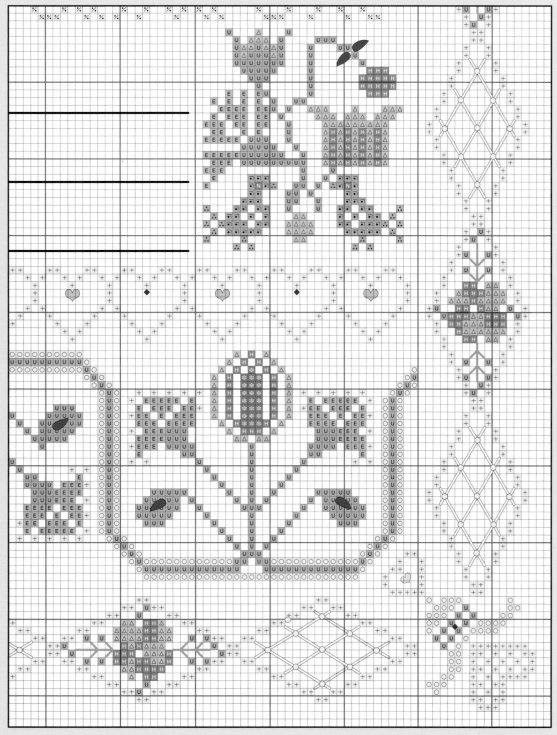

Bottom Right

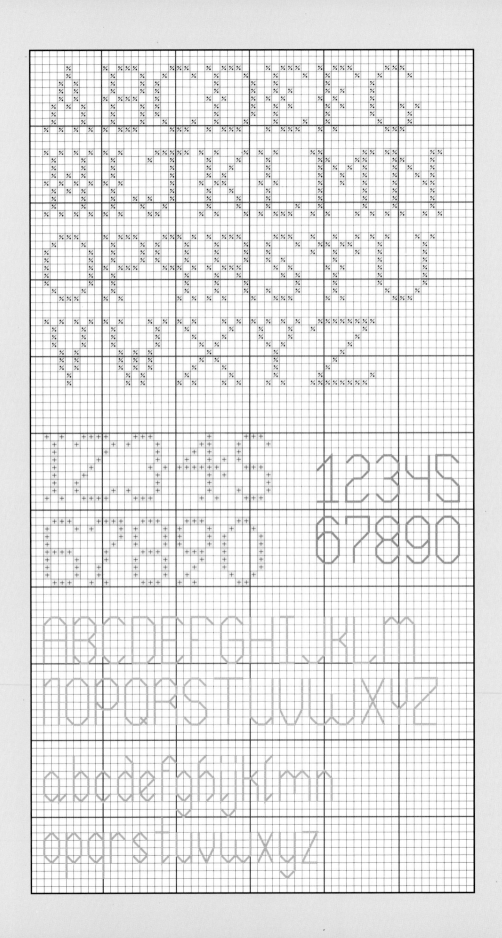

How Do I Combine Stitching Over One Thread and Over Two Threads on Linen in One Design?

Combining stitching over one thread and over two threads is done to give added detail to a particular section of a design. It is often done on faces. Stitching over one thread creates more detail on linen and allows for smoother color transition. In this example, it is used on violas to get a finer blend of color.

Le Jardin

Here's How:
Separate graphs are provided for over one thread and over two threads sections. Each grid square on either graph represents one stitch.

Note: Stitching over one thread results in a smaller design, or stitching twice as many stitches to cover the same area as when stitching over two threads.

Vertical Overthreads
The most common counting error when cross-stitching on linen is miscounting by one single linen thread.

It is helpful when counting on linen to begin stitching next to a vertical overthread. A vertical overthread is a warp thread that is on top of a weft thread. The diagram below illustrates a completed cross-stitch which began in the lower left hole adjacent to a vertical overthread.

If you bring your needle up from the back of the fabric in this manner, you will be able to easily check your needle placement with each and every stitch.

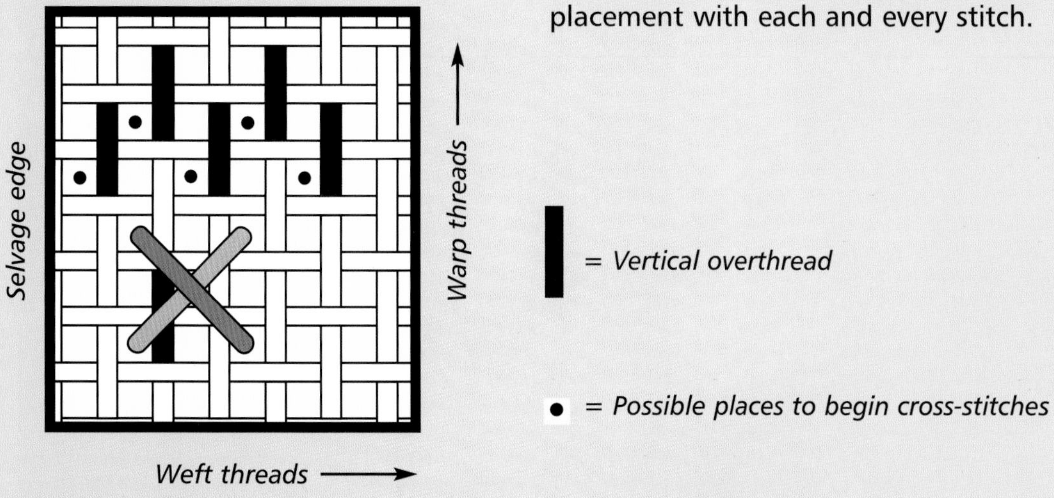

What You Need to Get Started:

Beads as indicated on graph
Cream sewing thread
Floss as indicated on graph
Linen
Paillettes as indicated on graph

Shown stitched on tea-dyed linen 28

Stitch Count:
61w x 123h

Design Size:
Aida 11 - 4½" x 7"
Aida 14 - 3⅝" x 5½"
Aida 18 - 2¾" x 4¼"
Linen 32 over 2 - 3⅛" x 4¾"

Selvage edge

Warp threads ⟶

Weft threads ⟶

▮ = *Vertical overthread*

● = *Possible places to begin cross-stitches*

Colonial Knot (CK)

1. From back of fabric, come up at 1. Drape floss in a backward "C" and place needle through "C".

2. Wrap floss over needle and under tip of needle forming a figure-8. Hold knot firmly on needle. Go down at 2. Hold floss securely until knot is formed on top of fabric.

Paillette Attachment (PA)

1. From back of fabric, come up at 1 and go down at 2. Come up at 3 and go down at 4. Come up at 5 and go down at 6.

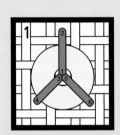

Paillette Attachment with Bead (PA/BD)

1. Use one strand of floss when attaching paillettes with beads. From back of fabric, come up at 1. String seed bead onto floss and go back down at 1.

Long-armed Cross (LAX)

1. From back of fabric, come up at 1 and go down at 2. Come up at 3 and go down at 4. Come up at 5 and go down at 6. Come up at 7 and go down at 8. Come up at 9 and go down at 10.

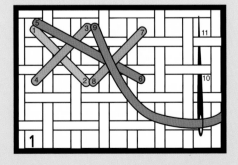

Rice Stitch (RS)

1. From back of fabric, come up at 1 and go down at 2. Come up at 3 and go down at 4.

2. Come up at 5 and go down at 6. Come up at 7 and go down at 8. Come up at 9 and go down at 10. Come up at 11 and go down at 12.

Tassel Outline (TO)

The tassel outline is a long stitch (see page 39).

Over Two Threads

1. Cross-stitch over two threads, using two strands of Mori unless otherwise indicated. When two colors are bracketed together, use one strand of each. Backstitch using one strand of Mori unless otherwise indicated.

2. For side borders, work rice stitch, using one strand Serica 7126 for bottom stitches and one strand Serica 7133 for top stitches.

3. Work colonial knot for poppy centers, using two strands.

4. Work long-armed cross-stitch, using one strand.

5. For Hungarian-point band, work satin stitches in direction of arrows, using one strand Serica 1092, 3013, 4162, 6124, and 7124 as indicated (see Diagram 1 on page 86).

Note: Diagram 1 illustrates one repeatable section of Hungarian-point band. Repeat this section until band is completed.

6. Work running backstitch for outline of roses, leaves, and small stems, using one strand cream sewing thread (see Diagrams 2 and 3 on page 87). Work satin stitch to fill roses,

using three strands Mori 1092, 1105, 3013, 3015, and 3021 as indicated, and a sharp needle, piercing linen threads of fabric when necessary to achieve a smooth appearance. Work satin stitch to fill leaves, using three strands of Mori 4164 and 4163 as indicated.

7. Couch one strand Japan thread #7 with one strand Japan thread #1 to cover sewing thread in design. Work straight stitch for rose thorns, using one strand very fine braid #4. Couch one strand very fine braid #4 with one strand Japan thread #1 to parallel rose stems and tendrils (see photo on page 84 for detail).

8. Work sawtooth satin-stitch border above "Le Jardin", using three strands (see page 73).

9. Backstitch outline of carnation petals, using one strand cream sewing thread. Work long

and short satin stitch to fill bottom half of carnation petals, using two strands Mori 3013 and fill top half of carnation petals, using two strands of Mori 3015 (see Diagram 4 on page 87).

10. For framework around violas, cross-stitch diamond frame, using one strand of very fine braid #4. Work straight stitch for latticework, using one strand Serica 7133.

Over One Thread
1. Cross-stitch violas over one thread, using one strand of floss.

Tassels
1. For center tassel, work horizontal satin stitch for tassel head, using one strand Serica 7126 (see Diagram 5 on page 88). Work vertical satin stitch for middle lines of tassel and outer lines of tassel head, using one strand

Diagram 1 — Top

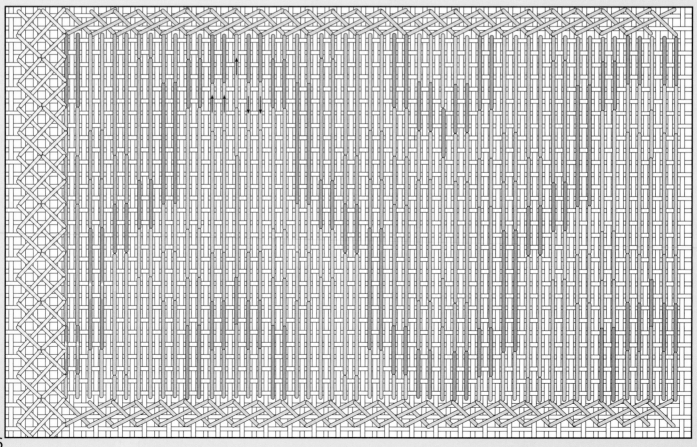

Serica 7126 (see Diagram 6 on page 88). Work vertical satin stitch for outer lines of tassel, using one strand Serica 7133. Work vertical satin stitch for inner lines of tassel and tassel head, using one strand Serica 7124. Work horizontal satin stitch for tassel neck, using one strand of Japan thread #7 (see Diagram 7 on page 88).

2. For side tassels, work vertical satin stitch for inner lines of tassels, using one strand Serica 7124. Work vertical satin stitch for middle lines of tassels, using one strand Serica 7126 (see Diagram 8 on page 88). Work vertical satin stitch for outer lines of tassels, using one strand Serica 7133. Work horizontal satin stitch for tassel neck, using one strand of Japan thread #7.

Diagram 2 — Top

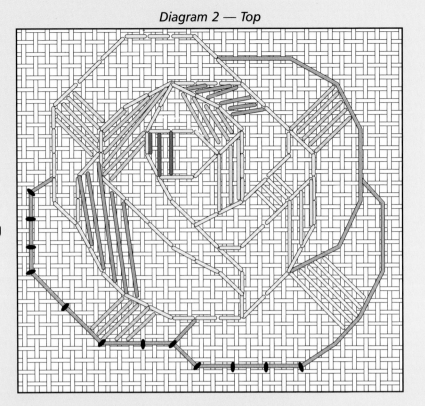

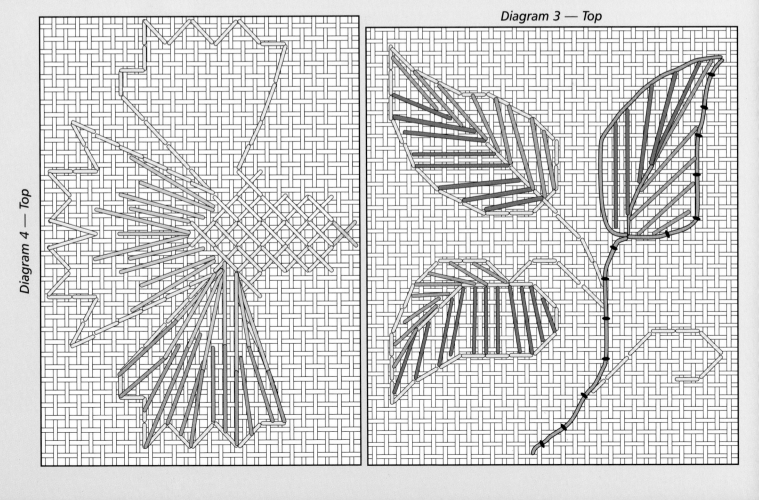

Diagram 4 — Top

Diagram 3 — Top

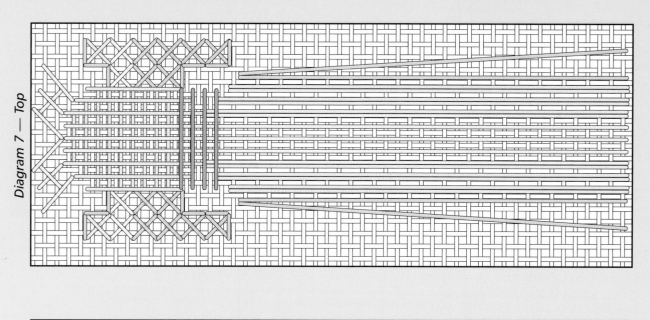

Diagram 7 — Top

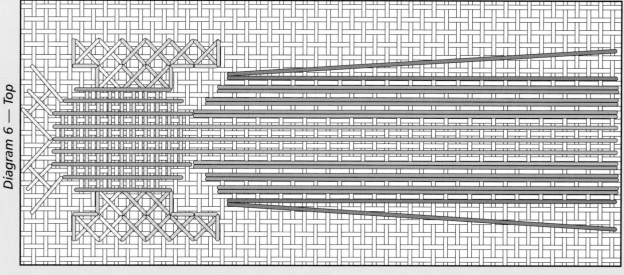

Diagram 6 — Top

Diagram 5 — Top

Diagram 8 — Top

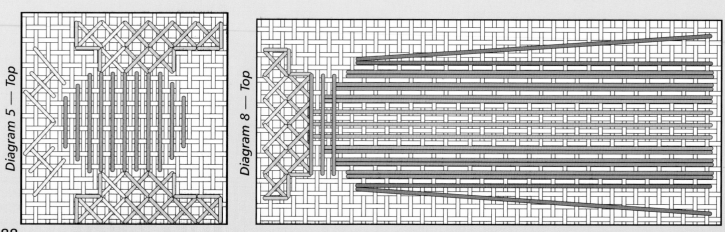

88

Kreinik Silk Mori

	XS	BS	CK	PA	PA/BD	LAX	RS	CT	SS	L/SSS	LS	UX	TO
3021 [−]									▥				
3013 [○]									▥	▯			
3015 [N]									▥	▯			
1105 [▨]									▥				
6104 [⊞]			●										
6106 [△]													
6083 [E]											╲		
4033 [Z]											╲		
4162 [✳]													
4163 [H]									▥				
4164 [▣]									▥		╲		
4166 [★]		⌐											
7133 [▨]		⌐				S			▥				
6106 / 6124 [U]		}											
6083 / 6126 [♥]		}											
7134 / 7135 [⊞]		}											
6126		⌐											
7134		⌐											
1092									▥				
*attach w/ 7133				◆									
03036 *attach w/ 6126 [◆]					⊙								
**002J													
***7126							✕						
***7133							◇						
***1092									▥	▯			
****#7 couch with #1								╱					
***7133											╲		
***7126												＋	
***7124										▯	╲		
***6124									▥				
***3013										▯			
***4162										▯			
See Instructions													⌐

*Kreinik Paillettes #14   **Kreinik Very Fine Braid #4
***Kreinik Silk Serica   ****Kreinik Japan Thread

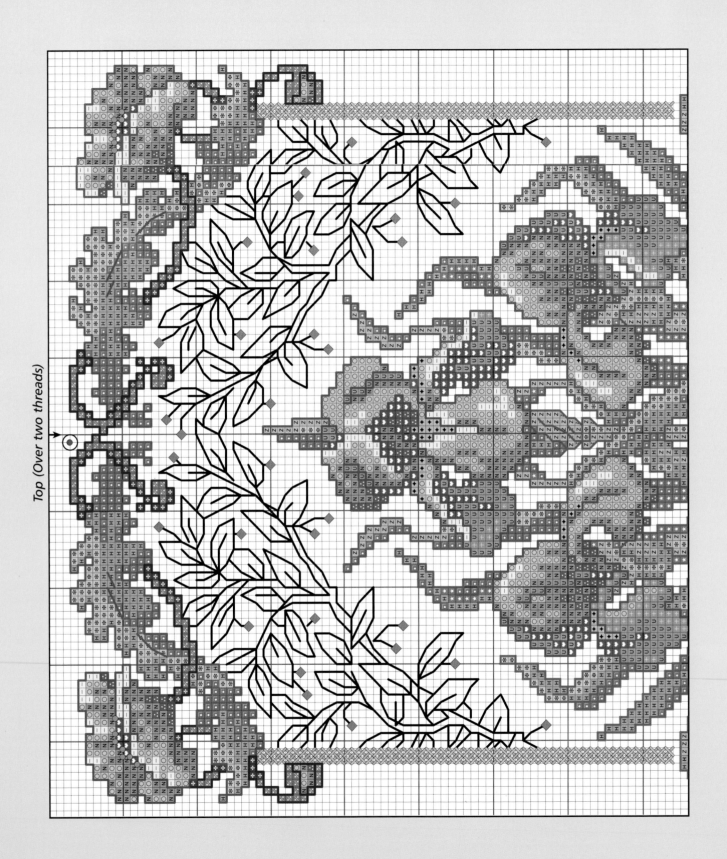

Top (Over two threads)

Middle (Over two threads)

Bottom (Over two threads)

Over one thread

94

Section 4: *gallery*

Emie Bishop

Designer Emie Bishop works from her farmhouse in the mountains of northern Utah. She fully expresses her appreciation and aptitude for many varieties of needlework, especially cross-stitch and Hardanger, into her designs. These designs have a distinctive "Emie" look to them—soft pastel florals with touches of heirloom lace. Her prestigious honors include five "Ginnie" Awards and nine People's Choice Awards.

Sharon Cohen

Designer Sharon Cohen of Germantown, Maryland, is a needlework artist who teaches and publishes her designs through her company, Nostalgic Needle. While her historic influences range from Renaissance costume to William Morris, she is particularly fond of Elizabethan embroidery. Formerly a freelance illustrator, her love of art and color began in early childhood with her first box of crayons.

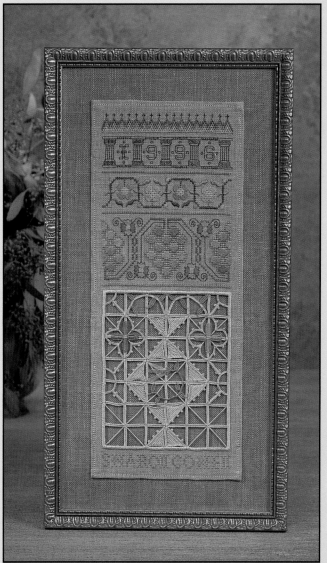

Janelle Giese

Designer Janelle Giese of Astoria, Oregon, began drawing as soon as she was old enough to pick up a pencil. As a child, her grandmother gave her colored pencils and paper to play with. However, her love for cross-stitching was a little slower to develop. Janelle became fascinated with cross-stitching while she was managing the craft and fabric department of a local department store. She was thrilled with the notion of "painting with needle and thread." She began learning to stitch and soon was entering competitions with her designs. She now has sold more than 260 cross-stitch and specialty embroidery designs, under the name Janelle Marie Designs as well as designing pieces for Kreinik.

Linda Gillum

Designer Linda Gillum is executive vice president and one of the founding members of Kooler Design Studio, Inc. Her whimsical teddy bear designs display an unmistakable style that has earned them the nickname "Linda Bears." Linda also specializes in coordinated baby ensembles and realistic depiction of animals. With a background in watercolors, oil painting, and pastels, she earned a fine art degree from the College of Arts and Crafts in Oakland, California, and is a Charted Designers of America Award winner.

LORD... MAKE ME AN
INSTRUMENT OF YOUR PEACE.
WHERE THERE IS HATRED, LET ME SOW LOVE...
WHERE THERE IS INJURY, PARDON...WHERE
THERE IS DOUBT, FAITH... WHERE THERE IS
DESPAIR, HOPE...WHERE THERE IS DARKNESS,
LIGHT AND WHERE THERE IS SADNESS, JOY.
St. FRANCIS

Tina and Teri Richards

Designer Tina Richards and her sister Teri Richards are co-owners of Shepherd's Bush, a needlework shop located in Ogden, Utah. The shop has been in business since 1984. In 1987, the sisters established a design business under the name Shepherd's Bush Printworks. Tina and Teri have had many European influences, including time spent as children in England with their grandmother. Tina attended the Univer-sity of Heidelberg, where she studied German history. These influences are apparent in her designs, which reflect a distinctive style of muted tones, un-usual color combinations, and charming "earth people."

Nancy Rossi

Designer Nancy Rossi, also a founding member of the Kooler Design Studio, Inc., uses her experience as an illustrator to create her distinctive needlework designs. These are noteworthy for their inventive, collage-style compositions. Her specialties include exquisite cat designs as well as needlepoint and crewel work, which allows her expertise as a colorist to shine. Also a potter, Nancy attended Syracuse University, New York.

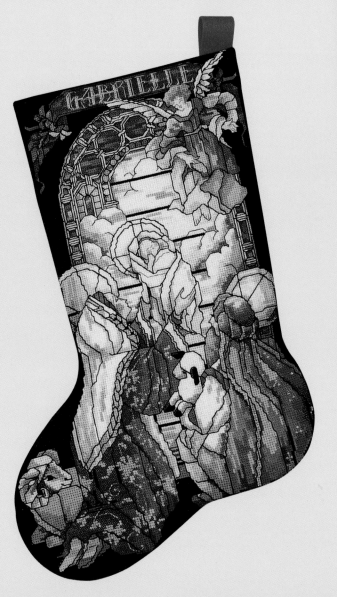

Anchor Conversion Chart

DMC	Anchor	DMC	Anchor	DMC	Anchor	DMC	Anchor
B5200	1	413	236	606	334	762	234
White	2	414	235	608	330	772	259
Ecru	387	415	398	610	889	775	128
208	110	420	374	611	898	776	24
209	109	422	372	612	832	778	968
210	108	433	358	613	831	780	309
211	342	434	310	632	936	781	308
221	897	435	365	640	393	782	308
223	895	436	363	642	392	783	307
224	893	437	362	644	391	791	178
225	1026	444	291	645	273	792	941
300	352	445	288	646	8581	793	176
301	1049	451	233	647	1040	794	175
304	19	452	232	648	900	796	133
307	289	453	231	666	46	797	132
309	42	469	267	676	891	798	146
310	403	470	266	677	361	799	145
311	148	471	265	680	901	800	144
312	979	472	253	699	923	801	359
315	1019	498	1005	700	228	806	169
316	1017	500	683	701	227	807	168
317	400	501	878	702	226	809	130
318	235	502	877	703	238	813	161
319	1044	503	876	704	256	814	45
320	215	504	206	712	926	815	44
321	47	517	162	718	88	816	43
322	978	518	1039	720	325	817	13
326	59	519	1038	721	324	818	23
327	101	520	862	722	323	819	271
333	119	522	860	725	305	820	134
334	977	523	859	726	295	822	390
335	40	524	858	727	293	823	152
336	150	535	401	729	890	824	164
340	118	543	933	730	845	825	162
341	117	550	101	731	281	826	161
347	1025	552	99	732	281	827	160
349	13	553	98	733	280	828	9159
350	11	554	95	734	279	829	906
351	10	561	212	738	361	830	277
352	9	562	210	739	366	831	277
353	8	563	208	740	316	832	907
355	1014	564	206	741	304	833	874
356	1013	580	924	742	303	834	874
367	216	581	281	743	302	838	1088
368	214	597	1064	744	301	839	1086
369	1043	598	1062	745	300	840	1084
370	888	600	59	746	275	841	1082
371	887	601	63	747	158	842	1080
372	887	602	57	754	1012	844	1041
400	351	603	62	758	9575	869	375
402	1047	604	55	760	1022	890	218
407	914	605	1094	761	1021	891	35

DMC	Anchor	DMC	Anchor	DMC	Anchor	DMC	Anchor
892	33	971	316	3688	75	3816	876
893	27	972	298	3689	49	3817	875
894	26	973	290	3705	35	3818	923
895	1044	975	357	3706	33	3819	278
898	380	976	1001	3708	31	3820	306
899	38	977	1002	3712	1023	3821	305
900	333	986	246	3713	1020	3822	295
902	897	987	244	3716	25	3823	386
904	258	988	243	3721	896	3824	8
905	257	989	242	3722	1027	3825	323
906	256	991	1076	3726	1018	3826	1049
907	255	992	1072	3727	1016	3827	311
909	923	993	1070	3731	76	3828	373
910	230	995	410	3733	75	3829	901
911	205	996	433	3740	872	3830	5975
912	209	3011	856	3743	869		
913	204	3012	855	3746	1030		

Variegated Colors

DMC	Anchor	DMC	Anchor	DMC	Anchor	DMC	Anchor
915	1029	3013	853	3747	120	48	1207
917	89	3021	905	3750	1036	51	1220
918	341	3022	8581	3752	1032	52	1209
919	340	3023	899	3753	1031	53	—
920	1004	3024	388	3755	140	57	1203
921	1003	3031	905	3756	1037	61	1218
922	1003	3032	898	3760	162	62	1201
924	851	3033	387	3761	928	67	1212
926	850	3041	871	3765	170	69	1218
927	849	3042	870	3766	167	75	1206
928	274	3045	888	3768	779	90	1217
930	1035	3046	887	3770	1009	91	1211
931	1034	3047	852	3772	1007	92	1215
932	1033	3051	845	3773	1008	93	1210
934	862	3052	844	3774	778	94	1216
935	861	3053	843	3776	1048	95	1209
936	846	3064	883	3777	1015	99	1204
937	268	3072	397	3778	1013	101	1213
938	381	3078	292	3779	868	102	1209
939	152	3325	129	3781	1050	103	1210
943	189	3326	36	3782	388	104	1217
945	881	3328	1024	3787	904	105	1218
946	332	3340	329	3790	904	106	1203
947	330	3341	328	3799	236	107	1203
948	1011	3345	268	3801	1098	108	1220
950	4146	3346	267	3802	1019	111	1218
951	1010	3347	266	3803	69	112	1201
954	203	3348	264	3804	63	113	1210
955	203	3350	77	3805	62	114	1213
956	40	3354	74	3806	62	115	1206
957	50	3362	263	3807	122	121	1210
958	187	3363	262	3808	1068	122	1215
959	186	3364	261	3809	1066	123	—
961	76	3371	382	3810	1066	124	1210
962	75	3607	87	3811	1060	125	1213
963	23	3608	86	3812	188	126	1209
964	185	3609	85	3813	875		
966	240	3685	1028	3814	1074		
970	925	3687	68	3815	877		

Kreinik Conversion Chart

DMC	Kreinik	DMC	Kreinik	DMC	Kreinik	DMC	Kreinik
Snow White	Blanc	356	4612	550	3336/3315	718	1043
Ecru	Creme/F2/F13	367	1835/3425	552	3314	720	634
208	1334/3335	368	1832/1842	553	3313	721	645
209	1342/3334	369	1841	554	3312	722	633
210	3334	370	2214	561	146	725	2514
211	3333	372	3833	562	144	726	522
221	4623/4624	400	4141/4215	563	143/211	727	2521
223	4622	402	632/2622	564	141	729	2234/2243/2533
224	4621	407	4611	580	516	730	3724
225	1011	413	3445	581	2124	731	516/2214
300	4142	414	3442	597	132	732	2124
301	2625	415	3441	598	1721/1723	733	2212
304	943/1026	420	526	602	3014	734	2212
307	543	422	3812	603	3013	738	3821/4112
309	2934/2945	433	4116/4122	604	3012	739	4241
310	Noir	434	4516	605	3021	740	624
311	1716	435	4236	606	915/935	741	611/624
312	1715	436	4235	608	635	742	545
315	4646	437	4234	610	3835	743	536
316	4634	444	536	611	4534	744	2532
317	3445	451	3414	612	3833	745	2542
318	3442	452	3413/3414	613	3832	746	2541
319	1845	453	3412/3413	632	4143	747	1723
320	1834	469	2125	640	3834	754	1012
321	941/943	470	245/2125	642	3713	758	2912
322	4922	471	2114	644	3422	760	2932/2943
326	1026	472	2122/2123	645	3844	761	1013/2931
327	3315	498	945/1026	646	3843	762	3441
333	1344	500	1846	647	1734	772	2113
334	1434	501	1844/3426	648	3841	775	1441
335	3014	503	1843	666	915/935	776	2941
336	1423	504	1822	676	2242	778	4631/4634
340	1343	517	1446/1725	677	2141	780	3816/3826
341	1433	518	1444	680	524	781	2516/3825
347	2924	519	1442	699	225	782	2244
349	915/935	520	3726	700	226	783	2244
350	914/934	522	1832/1842	701	235	791	1345
351	924	523	1841	702	224/236	793	4913
352	932/933	524	3423	703	223	794	1434
353	921/2913	535	3844	704	221	796	116
355	2636	543	3431	712	Brut	797	4924

DMC	Kreinik	DMC	Kreinik	DMC	Kreinik	DMC	Kreinik
798	4923	904	2116	971	633	3348	2113
799	4922	905	224	972	544/545	3350	3025
800	4921	906	223	973	536	3354	3021/3011
801	4115	907	244	975	4215	3362	3726
806	126	909	225	976	4212	3363	1832/1833
807	125	910	226	977	611/2546	3364	1831/3723
809	1434	911	214	986	1845	3371	4136
813	1443	913	213	987	2116	3609	1312
814	2926/4625	917	1043	988	2115	3685	3026
815	2925	918	4142	989	234	3687	3023/3024
816	946	919	2636	991	1826	3688	1042
817	916	920	2625	992	5013	3689	3031
818	2942	921	2615	993	1823	3705	914/934
819	1011	922	644	995	114	3706	932
820	116	924	205	996	113	3708	1021/1022
822	3711/3811	926	1745	3011	516	3712	2914
823	163/1425	927	1744	3012	2124	3713	1011
824	115	928	1742	3013	3722	3716	3021
825	1446	930	1715	3021	3846	3726	4645
826	113	931	1714	3022	3715	3727	3031
827	1442	932	1712	3023	3422	3731	3013
828	1721	934	3726	3024	3421/3841	3733	3012
829	526	935	2126	3031	4115	3743	3322
830	2214	936	2136	3032	4534	3746	1343
831	2214	937	516	3033	3711	3747	4911
832	2235	938	4124	3041	4635	3750	1716
833	2233	939	165	3042	4633	3752	1712
834	2242	945	2632	3045	3742	3755	112
838	4124	946	634	3046	2231	3760	1445
839	3433	948	2911	3047	2541/2542	3761	1722
840	3345/3434	950	2912	3051	2126	3765	126
841	3341	951	4241	3052	3723	3766	125
842	3431/4531	954	143/211	3053	3722	3768	1745
844	3844/3846	955	141	3064	4611	3770	F13
869	526	956	1024	3072	111/1813	3772	4611
890	1836/1845	957	1022	3078	2521	3774	2911
891	914	958	5013	3325	4921	3776	644
893	1014	959	5012	3326	3021	3778	2642
894	1022	961	3013	3328	2915	3779	2912
895	1845	962	3022	3340	912	3787	3344
898	4131/4124	963	2942	3341	911	3799	3445
899	2933	964	5011	3345	2116		
900	635/636	966	142	3346	2115		
902	2926/4626	970	634	3347	2114		

Metric Conversion Chart

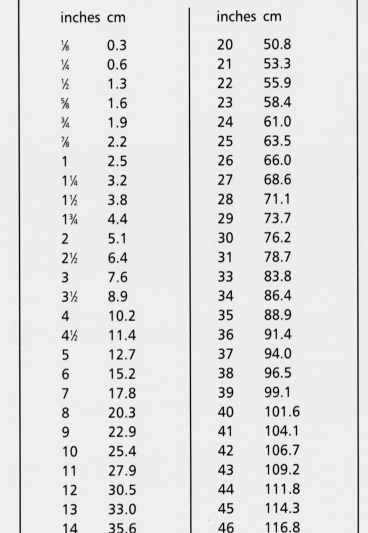

cm—Centimetres
Inches to Centimetres

inches	cm	inches	cm
⅛	0.3	20	50.8
¼	0.6	21	53.3
½	1.3	22	55.9
⅝	1.6	23	58.4
¾	1.9	24	61.0
⅞	2.2	25	63.5
1	2.5	26	66.0
1¼	3.2	27	68.6
1½	3.8	28	71.1
1¾	4.4	29	73.7
2	5.1	30	76.2
2½	6.4	31	78.7
3	7.6	33	83.8
3½	8.9	34	86.4
4	10.2	35	88.9
4½	11.4	36	91.4
5	12.7	37	94.0
6	15.2	38	96.5
7	17.8	39	99.1
8	20.3	40	101.6
9	22.9	41	104.1
10	25.4	42	106.7
11	27.9	43	109.2
12	30.5	44	111.8
13	33.0	45	114.3
14	35.6	46	116.8
15	38.1	47	119.4
16	40.6	48	121.9
17	43.2	49	124.5
18	45.7	50	127.0
19	48.3		

Index